F**k

An irreverent history of the F-word

RUFUS LODGE

F**k

An irreverent history of the F-word

The Friday Project
An imprint of HarperCollins*Publishers*
77–85 Fulham Palace Road
Hammersmith, London W6 8JB
www.harpercollins.co.uk

First published by The Friday Project in 2013
Copyright © Rufus Lodge 2013

3

Rufus Lodge asserts the moral right to be identified as the author of this work

A catalogue record for this book
is available from the British Library

ISBN 978-0-00-752200-2

Typeset in Minion by Palimpsest Book Production Ltd, Falkirk, Stirlingshire
Printed and bound in Great Britain by Clays Ltd, St Ives plc

MIX
Paper from
responsible sources
FSC™
www.fsc.org   **FSC˚ C007454**

Contents

Introduction: Why The F**k Do We Swear?   vii

1   ORIGINS   1
2   EXTENSIONS   21
3   EXCURSIONS   51
4   BAPTISMS   63
5   MOTHERS   79
6   EMBARRASSMENTS   95
7   SHOWCASES   117
8   PROHIBITIONS   139
9   IMPOSTERS   161

    Appendix   177
    Discography   187
    Acknowledgements   195

Introduction

Surveys of the British population claim that the nation's favourite words are 'serendipity', 'nincompoop', and – isn't this sweet? – 'love'. But there is another kind of love in this country, which dares not speak its name; and that's the love for another word with just four letters, but an entirely different meaning. It's been with us since the Middle Ages, it's as British as curry and chips, it rolls off the tongue of the average English-speaker with impressive frequency and ease, and it is surely, in our heart of hearts, the Great British Public's eternal favourite: the expletive known, and treasured, as the F-word.

It's a word from which I was shielded during my sheltered upbringing in an English country village – only to be shocked into brutal awareness when I moved to a large town. Through my early teens, it was still a word used only by other people. But by the time I was ready to leave school, greet the world, and hit the big city, I was as fluent as any docker or sailor in the land. Since then, the trusty F-word has been my companion in times of jubilation or despair, comfort or stress, endlessly adaptable, permanently relevant, and emotionally supportive in the way that only the truest of friends can be.

As you will see from the pages of this book, the F-word is also the most powerful word in our language, capable of arousing outrage and panic among the greatest in the land. So potent is its force, in fact, that when it explodes unexpectedly, it's known as the F-bomb, the mortal enemy of live TV and radio presenters around the world. It has inspired poetry and pornography, political protest and potty-mouthed pandemonium, and lots of things that don't begin with the letter 'p'. Take your seats, please, for a panoramic 500-year journey through the origins, adventures, and sexual liaisons of Britain's favourite word. You'll marvel at its versatility; thrill to its battles with the censors; revel in its unexpected appearances in the most embarrassing places; and, I hope, come away with a richer understanding of what makes that four-letter explosive so appealing, and so all-pervasive. You'll also learn some new swear-words. And abbreviations. WTF else do you people want?

Why the F**k Do We Swear?

Scientists – yes, real ones, with 'professor' and 'doctor' in front of their names – agree that swearing is good for you. Or, at least, it's good for you when you're stressed, under physical attack or have someone with 'professor' or 'doctor' in front of their names telling you to put your hands into icy water and keep them there.

That was the experiment run at Keele University, where Dr Richard Stephens discovered that people who shouted swear-words, notably the F-word, could keep their hands in the killingly cold water for 40 seconds longer than those who were only allowed to say 'My fingers have just fallen off'. The most effective thing to shout, almost certainly, was: 'Fuck, that's cold!', though 'Fucking scientists!' came in a close second.

Over to Dr Stephens for the conclusions inspired by this legalised torture: 'Used in moderation, swearing can be an effective and readily available short-term pain reliever if, for example, you are in a situation where there is no access to medical care or painkillers. However, if you're used to swearing all the time, our research suggests you won't get the same effect.' Which is bad news for Gordon Ramsay.

Why is this so? 'Swearing seems to activate deeper parts of the brain more associated with emotions,' according to Dr Stephens. These areas are different from those that control the normal production of language. As a result, it has been possible for people to suffer a catastrophic brain injury, which has left them unable to carry out a conversation, without impairing their ability to eff and blind like the proverbial supertrooper. (Research is still continuing into what happens in the brain to cause outbursts of uncontrollable swearing among a minority of sufferers from Tourette's syndrome.)

It's time for another scientist: Professor Yehuda Baruch of the University of East Anglia, who declared in 2007 that swearing can 'reflect solidarity and enhance group cohesiveness'. In other words, if one person in a group swears, and others feel some kind of bond with him, then they are likely to swear too. Not that this will be a surprise to anyone who's ever stood in the crowd at a football match.

One last scientific fact: by accessing an area of the brain left untouched by more delicate language, swearing provides a form of catharsis, bypassing the usual restraints of polite conversation. So swearing relieves stress, and helps to ease the experience of pain. But why do English-speakers, who have an array of foul language at their disposal, almost universally agree that the most satisfying and cathartic form of swearing has to involve the F-word and its various derivatives?

Here we must leave human biology and head into the realms of psychology. What does the word 'fuck' convey? Sex, simply enough; and, beyond that, a degree of violence. 'Fuck' is a much more aggressive term than 'have sex' or 'make love': it can be consensual (between two saucy so-and-so's who say to each other, 'Let's fuck') but it can also be directly the opposite ('I'm going to fuck you up'). It breaks two of society's strongest taboos, and multiplies the impact of both misdemeanours by combining them.

Taboos don't exist in isolation: they need a group of people to decide that something is beyond the pale, and then respect that decision. The English-speaking world has chosen to accept the F-word as one of the most offensive terms in its language. As expletives, 'flip' and 'fuck' perform exactly the same function, but only one of them is like to raise your maiden aunt's eyebrows. The boundaries of taboo can change: for centuries, any reference to God's wounds (those suffered by Jesus on the cross, in other words) enjoyed terrifying cultural power. Now 'zounds' survives only as an exclamation in comedy sketches about the Three Musketeers. But for more than 600 years 'fuck' has remained outside the realms of common decency – and only in the last fifty years has it slowly crept into the mainstream of our culture, to the point where some (but by no means all) newspapers and magazines will dare to print the four forbidden letters in full.

'Fuck' is also one of the most adaptable and multi-purpose words in the English dictionary, giving it a universal power that is denied to the C-word or the increasingly *verboten* N-word. It's also, strangely, an equal-opportunity four-letter word. No races, genders, or minorities are singled out by its use: it divides the world easily into two groups, those who say 'fuck' and those who find it shocking. Some people step backwards and forwards between those two categories – the men who swear in the office or in the pub, for instance, but hate to hear the F-word being used 'in front of the ladies'; or the parents who damn each other to hell, but drag their children away from the telly when Gordon Ramsay's producer is shouting down his earpiece that he hasn't said 'fuck' enough times yet.

'Fuck' is, when you get down to it, just a word like any other. But, at the same time, it's different from every other word you know. Pour boiling water over your fingers, and you'll soon remember why.

Origins

F.U.C.K.? No!

It is true that F.U.C.K. is an abbreviation for the phrase For Unlawful Carnal Knowledge. But it is not true that this abbreviation is the source of the word 'fuck'. Neither, for that matter, is another phrase that spells out the same unseemly word: Fornication Under Consent of the King.

Both phrases have a legal ring to them, and the hint that they might belong to bygone centuries, and so a pair of urban myths has grown up around the pair of them, in tandem. The explanations that their supporters employ are long and imaginative, but they boil down to a single, gristly core: that men in medieval authority grew so tired of writing out the phrase in question that it was abbreviated to save their time and their quills, and the condensed version survived long after the ancient civil service jargon was no longer relevant.

For Unlawful Carnal Knowledge was supposed to have been given as an explanation, in official papers and parchments, whenever a case of adultery was discovered and charged. It has even been claimed that the phrase, or its abbreviation, would be written across the stocks when a philanderer was facing the wrath of the people. Not true: adultery may indeed have been a crime in the past, but never under that name.

At the other extreme, some people were supposed to have been given a special licence to have sexual intercourse, or to produce babies: to these lucky souls, so the theory goes, was given permission for Fornication Under Consent of the King. You have to admit that this is a particularly attractive idea: it's easy to imagine the heraldic symbols belonging to the King's 1st Regiment of Shaggers. But, sadly, it's another invention.

Not that this prevented the rock band Van Halen from prolonging the myth that Carnal Knowledge was the root of the illicit F-word. In a burst of adolescent bravado, the band decided in 1999 to call their next album *Fuck*. Once they had been informed that this would prevent the record being sold at almost all retail outlets, they fell back on the old canard about the punishment of adulterers, and named their album after the phrase that spelled out F.U.C.K. Their information may have been way off beam, but not their commercial instincts, as the record reached the top of the American charts. This proved conclusively that none of the buyers at the nation's biggest and most conservative retail chains – usually primed to slap a sales ban on anything that might corrupt the innocent masses of Middle America – was capable of recognising a blatant reference to the F-word when it was placed in front of them.

Channel Crossing

Some of our rudest words can be traced back to those dirty Anglo-Saxons, who seem to have had an anal fixation a full millennium before this crucial stage of child development was first identified. Not content with beating each other over the head with cudgels and writing *Beowulf*, they made several fundamental contributions to our native tongue. It's the lads in helmets whom we have to thank for such earthy terms as 'shit', 'turd', 'fart', and 'arse' – sparking the 1,300-year-long obsession with potty language that has made us the great nation we are today.

Enter the French. William's conquerors may have invaded the country, killed our king, immortalised the battle in a wide-screen (tapestry) epic, and written down all our assets in a big book with a gloomy title; but apart from that, what did the Normans ever do for us? Well, they taught us how to 'piss': we must have been desperate to go by the time they arrived.

After the French, things became more confused: the natives were too busy cooking onion soup and composing *chansons* to keep track of what was happening to England's glorious tongue. Those scholars who love wallowing around in the pre-history of foul language, and then have to compile entire dictionaries of more respectable words to disguise their bad habits, are generally agreed that some of our most traditional curse words, such as 'bum', 'cunt', and 'twat', have origins that are, to say the least, rather muddy. Some people would like to place the blame on visitors from Scandinavia, Holland, or Germany, but they all have alibis for the night in question, which leaves us none the clearer.

So it won't surprise you that none of these filthy foreigners is prepared to own up and admit responsibility for creating the king of our four-letter words. So let's examine what we know for sure. 'Fuck' (or 'fucke' or 'fuk' or 'fukk' – the same people who thought the Earth was flat weren't very good at spelling, either) was definitely a part of our language before 1598, which is when John Florio, the original Englishman abroad, compiled his Italian-English dictionary, *A Worlde of Wordes*. He defined the Italian verb 'fottere' as meaning 'to iape, to sard, to fucke, to swive, to occupy'. Florio soon became the English tutor of Queen Anne of Denmark, and it's intriguing to wonder how many of those words he taught her before she made any state visits to the British Isles (and also whether he told her what they really meant).

When I said 'our' language above I was being deliberately vague. The prime exponents of the F-word during the sixteenth century were the Scots, which won't surprise anyone who's ever watched a Celtic vs. Rangers derby at close quarters. Indeed, they are responsible for all of its pre-Florio appearances on paper. But nowhere even in the distant history of the English tongue is there any suggestion that 'fuck' first landed in Scotland, and then surreptitiously made its way south, quickly corrupting Newcastle and Liverpool before finally reaching Eastbourne in about 1973. So we can only assume that, for obscure social reasons, Scots were less embarrassed about using the already taboo word than their English counterparts.

None of which helps us to discover where we – Scottish or English – picked up such a dirty word. Given that our Anglo-Saxon heritage brought us so much earthy filth, it would be easy to imagine that 'fuck' came from the same source. But the Angles and Saxons seem to have been too busy farting to worry about copulation. So, with no evidence of 'fuck' pre-dating the French, is it possible that William's lads didn't just conquer us but also perverted our vocabulary? Here there is the partial evidence of the French verb 'foutre' (sometimes rendered in the past as 'foutra'), which comes from the Latin 'futuere' – both describing the action of sexual congress.

That might explain the 'fu–' of 'fuck', but where could the '–ck' come from? Enter the historians who stake the case for the German influence – specifically the verb 'ficken' (meaning 'to strike', a theme that crops up in several English sex verbs between 1400 and 1800). But though logic might suggest that 'fuck' was therefore a French/German hybrid, words don't evolve that way, with a polite sharing of letters from two different sources to create something new: like the armies that spoke them, languages tend to fight to the finish, knocking out their opponents and establishing themselves on their vanquished turf with all their letters intact.

In any case, there's a third strand to consider: from Scandinavia. Old Norse pretty much ruled the roost over all of that territory in the years after William the Conqueror shouted out 'Harold, is that a bird or a plane?' and the king of England got an arrow in his eye. And in Old Norse there's a verb that both sounds and looks like a close cousin of our own faithful F-word – 'fukja', meaning 'to drive' (as in the sense of chasing things around, rather than getting stuck in a six-lane contraflow on the M1). Two words of Scottish dialect, 'windfucker' and 'fucksail', seem to confirm that 'fukja' did cross the North Sea to Aberdeen and Dundee, although neither of them has the slightest hint of profanity about it.

But wait: here's a fourth contender, from another land entirely. Not content with creating Edam cheese, the inhabitants of Holland concocted Middle Dutch, a collection of related dialects that left their mark on Germany as well. Hiding among the multiple terms for clogs and windmills (though very few for mountains) was 'fokken' – a verb that meant exactly what it sounds like, widening its terms very quickly (by linguistic standards) from a word for 'thrust' to one that implied one person thrusting something into another.

Case closed, then? Not entirely. Because while the Dutch were busy 'fokken', those Scandinavians were keeping themselves warm during the long Nordic winters by developing their own tongues (and not like that). At around the same time, the word 'fukka' cropped up in Norway; and 'focka' in Sweden, where there was also a noun, 'fock', for the male organ.

So what seems to have happened is that what became known

as Great Britain was surrounded by foreigners, all of whom were inventing their own words for sexual intercourse while the Brits were still swapping fart jokes. And during the fifteenth century, one or more of those illegal immigrants crossed the waters and started showing our innocent lads and lasses that there was something in life even more fun than having a poo. 'What's that called?' asked our medieval Gavin and Stacey. And so Britain fell in love with an imported word that, like German lager and Indian food, has become so central a part of our culture that we prefer to think it was ours from the beginning.

Some Word There Was, Blacker Than Tybalt's Death . . .

'A word,' Shakespeare's characters are wont to say, as they beg a moment of their companion's time. But surely one word was forbidden even to this most vocabulary-rich of writers? Could the Immortal Bard really have resorted to the basest of language to please the filthy ears of the theatre-goers at the pit of the Globe?

Several early editions of his work suggest that he could, and did. Not the F-word, as such, but a six-letter term for someone in the very act of fornication – and not with a timeless heroine, a Cleopatra or a Juliet, but with a more humble member of God's kingdom: the common British rabbit.

The offending text, if offence it should cause, could be found in *Henry IV Part 1*, Act II, Scene iv, in the voice of the one Shakespearian character whom it is possible to imagine effing and blinding in the wings: that buffoonish gourmet and glutton, Falstaff. At which point I refer you to the 1778 edition of Shakespeare's collected plays: in which Falstaff appears to dare his king to 'hang me up by the heels for a rabbet-fucker, or a poulter's hare'. The editor has inserted a helpful footnote from no less an

8

authority than lexicographer extraordinaire, Dr Samuel Johnson: '"Rabbet-fucker" is, I suppofe, a fucking rabbet.' (By the same logic, Dr Johnson would doubtless have explained that a 'mother-fucker' was actually a fornicating matriarch.)

But, as Hamlet says to Laertes, 'I have done you wrong', sweet Bard. The clue is in that mysterious 'suppofe': there, as in the offending rabbit reference, a sinless 's' has been printed as a fallacious 'f', translating a sucking rabbit (or someone who makes a habit of sucking these innocent furry creatures) into a fornicating example of the same mammal. A veritable comedy of errors, my lord.

How, you might ask, did the Bard convey the sense of the F-word without descending to such common tongue? By referring to an 'act', on occasion, as an abbreviation (though not too abbreviated, one hopes, for Juliet's sake) of the enactment of copulation. On two occasions, however, Shakespeare was cunning enough a linguist to suggest the forbidden term whilst still being able to swear innocent intent.

The first returns us, inevitably, to the company of Falstaff, in the same play in which he debates the rearing habits of the rabbit. Near the climax of the drama, he is engaged in heated conversation with the aptly named Pistol, a hothead who is much given to letting rip with his own command of invective. Where his twenty-first-century equivalent might cry, 'I don't give a fuck about . . .', Pistol opts for the safety of a foreign language, in this instance French, while still giving his monolingual audience enough of the F-sound to make his meaning entirely clear. So let's hear him in action: 'A foutra for the world and worldlings base!' And, a few lines further: 'A foutra for thine office'. Pistol certainly can't be accused of going off half-cock. (For an entire scene devoted to the build-up to a 'foutra' joke, meanwhile, try *Henry V*, III. iv.)

F**k

Sir John Falstaff was also in the cast of Shakespeare's second foray into F-word euphemism, in *The Merry Wives of Windsor*, IV.i. But for once he is out of the room when Sir Hugh Page, a Welsh parson of less learning than he assumes, gives the leading characters a break by quizzing young William Page about his knowledge of Latin grammar. Having led him through the pitfall-free ground of the nominative and accusative cases, he asks the boy to provide him with the 'focative'. Good scholar that he is, William corrects him: 'O, vocativo'. But Sir Hugh ploughs on with his 'foc'-word, setting up Mistress Quickly for a particularly limp pun about a carrot. By the time that Sir Hugh moves on to the genitive case, the coarser element of the Elizabethan audience would doubtless have been in hysterics – repeating 'He said "focative"!' and 'Ha, ha! "Genitive"!' to each other like schoolboys who'd just learned Monty Python's parrot sketch. Fortunately, as keen viewers of BBC3 will tell you, modern comedy is much more sophisticated.

Poetry in Flyte

It was, perhaps, the Renaissance equivalent of battle rap: two skilled artisans in the arts of insult and verse, flinging lines back and forth for the entertainment of a rabid crowd. This was not a beer-soaked hip-hop club on Detroit's 8 Mile Road, however, but a rowdy evening at the court of King James IV of Scotland, circa 1500. The monarch would assemble his courtiers, and let loose two of his sharpest wordsmiths to heap invective and obscenity on each other's head.

The result was a jolly good flyting, a word that promised scolding and wrangling with the overtones of violence. As the audience was hand-picked by the King, there were no holds barred

– with the result that the strenuous *Flyting of Dumbar and Kennedie* has passed into history as the earliest known printed text to include one of the rudest words in the Scottish (and English) language.

The two participants were William Dunbar and his slightly older but less celebrated opponent, Walter Kennedy. Dunbar was the man who would go down in literary history, the Ali to Kennedy's Frazier; but it was the lesser-ranked fighter who was credited in the 1507 anthology of Dunbar's verse with calling his antagonist a 'fantastic fule' and 'ignorant elf' to warm himself up, before delivering his killer lines: 'Skaddit shaitbird and common shamelar/Wanfukkit funling that Natour maid ane yrle'. Which translates, roughly, as 'Mangy rascal and common scrounger/ Misbegotten [wanfukkit, or produced by an unhappy act of intercourse] foundling that Nature made a midget'.

Dunbar wasn't a man to let that kind of thing stand unanswered, of course, and he quickly replied with some delicious lines alleging that Kennedy was both 'cuntbitten' and 'beschitten'. Ah, the magic of poetry . . .

What isn't clear is how these insults were recorded for posterity, the court of James IV being intolerably ill-supplied with cassette recorders or iPhones. Did the King's retinue include the speediest scribe in the land? Did both men actually arrive with their anger pre-cooked, and merely pass over their manuscripts to an editor at the end? Or did Dunbar, in fact, cook up the whole stew himself, thereby entitling himself to sole credit for the results? History does not tell us. Nor, after the sixteenth century, did collections of verse dare to reproduce the most extreme of the two poets' slingshots in full: 'wanfukkit' was quietly censored to read 'wanthriven'; 'cuntbitten' revised as 'flaebittin', suggesting that those midges were every bit as annoying four hundred years ago as they are today.

Grose Vulgarity

Of all the lexicographers, etymologists, encyclopedics, and anoraks who have devoted their lives to chronicling the English language at its most blunt and disorderly, the award for displaying the most conspicuous courage in dictionary corner must go to Francis Grose. Aptly named, you might think, and the surviving engraving of his friendly form does suggest that he was the answer to the oft-voiced question, 'Who ate all the pies?'. But Grose deserves every credit for his lifelong quest to bring recherché knowledge into the public eye. He penned comprehensive (for the late eighteenth century) volumes devoted to sites where antiquities might be found; to the history of armour and weaponry; and to local proverbs gathered from every nook and cranny of the British Isles.

His enduring monument, though, was his *Classical Dictionary of the Vulgar Tongue*, first published in 1785 and reprinted many times thereafter – although as the boundaries of good taste narrowed during the nineteenth century, later editions tended to remove some of Grose's more daring entries.

From the start, he was prepared for outrage from the disgusted citizens of the newly fashionable resort of Tunbridge Wells. 'To prevent any charge of immorality being brought against this work,' he declared in his introduction, 'the Editor begs leave to observe that when an indelicate or immodest word has obtruded itself for explanation, he has endeavoured to get rid of it in the most decent manner possible; and none have been admitted but such, as could not be left out, without rendering the work incomplete.' Couldn't have said it better myself.

Daring though Grose was in the collecting of his vulgar language, there were some words that still had to be hidden beneath a veil of modesty. Most extreme was ****, which could not even be included in the alphabetical dictionary without revealing its identity. But Grose did offer some clues: a 'nincompoop', he declared, was 'one who never saw his wife's ****'; while a gentleman who entered a woman without sparing any of his vital fluids could be said to have 'made a coffee house out of a woman's ****'. Not that Grose was exactly short of synonyms for a woman's mysterious ****. Among them were her 'bite', 'bumbo' (as used, apparently, by 'Negroes'), 'Carvel's ring', 'cauliflower', 'cock alley', 'cock lane', 'commodity', 'dumb glutton', 'gigg', 'madge' (has Madonna been told?), 'mantrap', 'money' (rather alarmingly, this was used only of young girls), 'muff' (oops, nearly given the game away), and 'notch'.

On special occasions, the woman's **** could be joined with the man's ****, or, in other words, his 'prick', 'tarse', or 'plug tail', kept fuelled by his 'bawbels', 'gingambobs', 'nutmegs', 'tallywags', 'tarrywags', and 'whirlygigs' (don't try that one at home). The act of union could be described (yes, even in 1785) as 'making the beast with two backs', 'making a buttock ball', doing a 'clickit' (as foxes do, noisily, at night), 'docking' (think space capsules), 'humping' (going out of fashion by the 1780s, we learn), 'joining giblets' (very romantic they were, in the late eighteenth century), 'creating a goats-gigg', 'strumming' or 'knocking' (a man did this to a woman), 'mowing' (but only in Scotland; in England, you better keep off the grass), 'screwing', 'wapping' (now we know why Rupert Murdoch based his newspapers there), or, most common of all in the years preceding 1800, 'swiving'. In order to prevent an unwanted outcome, a man might choose to 'fight in armour' by wearing a 'c-d-m' (that's a 'cundum' to you and me, sir).

Some gentlemen preferred not to bother with the ladies at all, and might fairly be described as a 'back gammon player', an 'indorser', 'a madge cull' (doing away with a 'madge', presumably), a 'shitten prick' (slightly too graphic, that one), or as frequenting the 'windward passage' (much more poetic).

If more solitary pleasure was intended, a man (but obviously never a woman) might 'frig' ('to be guilty of the crime of self-pollution'), 'get cockroaches' (maybe I'm doing it wrong), 'box the Jesuit' (likewise), or 'mount a corporal and four' (the corporal is the thumb, and you can work out the rest for yourselves). Once he'd tired of playing by himself, the man could entice the lower class of woman to perform 'bagpipes' upon him ('a lascivious practice too indecent for explanation'), give him a good 'huffle' ('a piece of beastiality too filthy for explanation', but strangely similar to that bagpipes manoeuvre), or even indulge him in a quick spasm of 'larking' ('a lascivious practice that will not bear explanation', even here, where I can only refer you to a modern dictionary and the word 'irrumation').

Many of Grose's definitions shine a surreal light upon the habits and prejudices of 1785, not least the three-and-a-half pages he devoted (in a dictionary!) to a diatribe against gypsies. He was greatly interested in the word 'dildo', defined thus: 'an implement resembling the virile member, for which it is said to be substituted, by nuns, boarding school misses, and others obliged to celibacy, or fearful of pregnancy'. These unusual objects 'are to be had at many of our toy shops and nick nackatories', though I wouldn't advise you to enquire at Toys R Us.

It's intriguing, to say the least, to discover that the eighteenth-century gentleman needed a phrase to describe 'a lighted candle stuck into the private parts of a woman', which was known as a 'burning shame'. Maybe the candle was an attempt to burn the disease out of a 'fireship' (a woman with a STI), who was suffering perhaps from 'French Disease' (damn those dirty frogs) or 'Drury Lane Ague' (known today as luvvie's syndrome). Of course, all that unpleasantness could be avoided by a 'flogging cully': 'one who hires girls to flog him on the posterior, in order to procure an erection' (the life of an architect was clearly not a happy one).

But you haven't come to the pages of this book for such trivia, I hear you say. So we move, at last, to the pages of the dictionary devoted to words beginning with the letter 'F', of which precisely two had to be abridged in the interests of public decency: 'f—k' (meaning 'to copulate', you will be startled to discover); and 'f—k beggar', which is of course a synonym for 'buss beggar'; you know, 'an old superannuated fumbler', fumbling in this instance suggesting that the architect's erection might be less sturdy than he was hoping. There was one further reference to our favourite word, in the appearance of 'duck f-ck-r', which Grose helpfully defined as 'the man who has the care of the poultry on board a ship of war' (no bestiality in the Navy, maties).

Of course, as keen lexicographers, you will be much more interested to know that, in Grose's alphabet, words beginning with 'I' and 'J' intermingled in a saucy manner, as if the two letters were interchangeable; and that 'V' came before 'U' (whereas a gentleman always makes sure that 'U' should come first).

Doctor in the House

Doctor Samuel Johnson is still revered today as the doyen of dictionary makers, despite – or perhaps because of – his refusal to countenance the inclusion of any language that he could not repeat in genteel society. Yet the doctor was not deaf to the existence of such terms. In a true meeting of eighteenth-century giants, Johnson was once asked by actor David Garrick to name the greatest pleasure in life. His reply, Garrick related, was 'fucking; and second was drinking. And therefore he wondered why there were no more drunkards, for all could drink, though all could not fuck.'

One of those who could undoubtedly do both was Johnson's

Boswell – the original Boswell of the cliché, in fact, who in his journals reported that a prostitute named Louise had congratulated him on the remarkable feat of achieving intercourse five times within a single night. This was, of course, James Boswell, who dogged the doctor's footsteps for several decades, committing all the great man's *aperçus et bons mots* to paper. He duly chronicled the 'fucking and drinking' quip, but (to the disappointment of students for centuries thereafter) elected not to include it in his epic *Life of Samuel Johnson*, reserving his multiple volumes for all the discussions in which the doctor triumphed over his interlocutors without resorting to the F-word.

All Over the Effing Place

(Some of) the Many Faces of the F-Word

FUCK: *verb* (intransitive)
To have sexual intercourse. 'I fuck as often as I can.'

FUCK: *verb* (transitive)
To have sexual intercourse with someone. 'I fuck my wife as often as I can.'

To damn or dismiss something or somebody: 'Fuck my wife!'

To exploit: 'If she asks for a divorce, I'm going to fuck her completely when it comes to a settlement.'

FUCK: *verb* (often with additions)
To mess things or people up: 'I'm going to fuck up my wife and fuck with her head for asking for a divorce.'

To make a mistake: 'I may have fucked up when I told her I fancied my secretary.'

FUCK: *noun*
The act of sexual intercourse: 'I caught my wife having a fuck with her lover.'

One thrust in the act of sexual intercourse: 'Then she said that he gave her one last enormous fuck, and she came. Again.'

Someone who has sexual intercourse: 'I'm the best fuck in town, despite what my wife may tell you.'

A bastard, a rascal: 'That guy who's fucking my wife is such a fuck.'

Something of no value: 'I couldn't give a fuck about that fucker.'

Something of some quantity: 'She says his organ is as big as fuck.'

FUCK: *exclamation* (often with additions)
An expression of contempt: 'Fuck off! What do you see in this guy?'

An expression of annoyance: 'Fuck! I saw him at the golf club. His penis is *huge!*'

An expression of surprise: 'Fuck me! How does he get it in his trousers?'

FUCKER: *noun*

Someone who has sexual intercourse: 'She says her lover is an amazing fucker . . .'

A bastard, a rascal: '. . .but he's just a complete fucker as far as I'm concerned.'

Something bad: 'She's leaving me for him. Isn't that a fucker?'

FUCKED: *adjective*

Pertaining to sexual intercourse: 'She said that for the first time in her life she felt utterly and completely fucked.'

Pertaining to exhaustion: 'And then she had the nerve to say, "We've done it so many times, I'm completely fucked".'

Pertaining to drink/drugs: 'I had so many vodkas to get over the shock that I was completely fucked.'

Pertaining to exploitation: 'She's getting fucked, and I'm left feeling fucked.'

Pertaining to mental derangement: 'She is totally fucked, going for this guy, just because he's great in bed. And has a huge penis. And an apartment in Nice. And a private jet.'

FUCKING: *noun*

An act of sexual intercourse: 'She says he's coming round again tonight, to give her a proper fucking.'

An act of exploitation: 'I'm paying the bills, he's screwing my wife, and I'm getting a good fucking.'

FUCKING: *participle*
Having sexual intercourse: 'I caught the pair of them, fucking on the new sofa. Where did we get it? Ikea, actually.'

FUCKING: *intensifying adjective*
Something negative and annoying: 'That sofa is fucking ruined.'

A sentence-filler that expresses extreme emotion: 'No one seems to want to go near it. I might as well chop the fucking thing off.'

Extensions

A Bit on the Side

Not content with its reputation as an all-purpose, linguistic assault weapon, the F-word also has a penchant for seeking out company. It has the power to transform the most innocent of words into verbal grenades, as these examples demonstrate . . .

ABSO-FUCKING-LUTELY: A prime example of what the linguists call 'infixation', in which one word insists on sitting right in the middle of another. Now you know what it's called, you can make up your own examples.

BUMBLEFUCK: 'Bumble' stands for 'bumbling idiot'; 'fuck' stands for everything that it usually does. So a 'bumblefuck' is a 'fucker' who is also an idiot: or an idiot, in other words. When applied to a situation, a bumblefuck is one that was probably designed by a whole circus of bumblefucks, and thus should be avoided wherever possible.

BUMFUCK: Forget the obvious definition, which is . . . yes, you've got it. A 'bumfuck' can also be a 'bum fuck': that is, someone with whom it is not much fun to share a sleeping bag. On the basis that someone's sexual etiquette is probably a reflection of their wider character, the word can also be applied to a person who is unpleasant with clothes on or off.

CLUSTERFUCK: A remarkably descriptive American term for a scene in which there are lots of people doing lots of unusual things with lots of other people, and none of them are wearing any undergarments. Fine as a fantasy, but actually rather annoying in real life, believe me. And so, by extension, it also applies to a situation that is extremely chaotic – but not actually that enjoyable.

FACEFUCK: At the risk of turning this into a sexual guidebook, 'facefuck' is a way of describing oral sex, particularly fellatio; and even more particularly if the person doing the sucking is lying on their back with an open mouth. Someone who is 'facefucked', however, is more likely in the twenty-first century to be 'off their face' having ingested something smaller, but probably more dangerous, in the way of drugs.

FINGERFUCK: A social activity in which a finger – or more: adjust according to taste – becomes an explorer, if you like, of dark caverns.

FLYING FUCKLAND: A more modern and less poetic way of saying 'Cloudcuckooland' – a place of fantasy that could surely not exist in real life. Editor's note: outside the pages of Erica Jong's novel *Fear of Flying*, a flying fuck is rarely a good thing.

FUCKAHOLIC: An alcoholic is addicted to alcohol; a workaholic never leaves the office; a fuckaholic will fuck you even if you're an alcoholic and a workaholic, because they simply don't care where they put themselves.

FUCK-AROUND: The phrase 'fuck around' probably doesn't need any explanation, unless you've just come out of a convent, in which case this book probably isn't the ideal place to start. Don't try *Fifty Shades of Grey*, either. The more jaded of you can read on. Someone who fucked around sometimes came to be called a fuck-around; and then, starting on the island of Fiji, the word was applied to anyone who happened to be hanging around in the streets, usually with criminal intentions.

FUCKARSE: Someone who is a bit of a prat. As opposed to FUCK ARSE, which does exactly what it says on the tin.

FUCKATHON: Someone who is a fuckaholic, or who takes fucking around to the extremes, might take part in a fuckathon. In commercial terms, 'fuckathon' has been used as another way of describing 'gang bang' pornography, in which a female porn star attempts to have intercourse with as many partners as possible in a specified period. The supremely unerotic film starring Annabel Chang, *The World's Biggest Gang Bang*, is the best possible advertisement against the fuckathon, which makes a clusterfuck seem like afternoon tea at the vicarage. Like Boy George, I'd rather have a cup of tea.

FUCKASS: An all-purpose term of abuse, which doesn't usually have any specific connection to anal activities.

FUCKBAG: Nearly as all-purpose as 'fuck' itself: it can be a noun, denoting someone with little common sense; or someone (usually a woman, surprise surprise) who is known for having lots of sex; or it can be an adjective; or an exclamation of despair or disgust. And you can use it as one word or two. Satisfied?

FUCKBALL: Another derogatory term, familiar from the movie *Get Shorty*. Over to you, Harvey Keitel: 'Fuck you, fuckball.'

FUCK-BAR: An establishment in which fucking takes place, or in which one secures the vital connection to enable the same thing. A pick-up joint, in other words. Coined by the American gay community in the 1970s, it's used for a bar with back-room reserved for all kinds of sporting activity.

FUCKBEANS: I'd love to report that this is a slang term for Viagra, because it clearly should be. But disappointingly it's a piece of youth-speak meaning nothing more than that the person who uses it is slightly cross.

FUCK-BEGGAR: Originally, a man with a reputation for not being able to raise the mast when the, er, 'boat' is about to set sail. More widely, anyone who is so desperate for a sexual partner that they have to beg. Alternative term in the eighteenth century: 'buss-beggar' (not to be confused with someone who gets on a bus with a sob story about having lost their money on the way to the bus stop, like the woman I always see in the South Ealing Road).

FUCK BOOK: A work of pornography, designed to provide sexual excitement. Unlike this book, which is strictly educational.

FUCKBOY: A male, usually young, and presumably not already gay, who finds himself the unwelcome recipient of attention from other males when he arrives in prison. The female equivalent, 'fuckgirl', doesn't seem to have come into such regular usage, perhaps because not all female prisons are like the ones in Hollywood porno movies.

FUCKBRAIN: A person whose brains have 'gone to fuck', and not because they want to have sex.

FUCK BUDDY: A friend with whom you have sex. In theory, this sex is wildly enjoyable, and totally free of complications and commitments. In practice, it usually buggers up the friendship. Though there was this one occasion I remember when [continued on page 316].

FUCK-CHOPS: See FUCKBRAIN. Proof that you can add almost anything to the word 'fuck' if you want to call someone a prat.

FUCK-DUST: A multipurpose word, which originated in the 1950s as a description of stuff that simply wasn't up to scratch. By the 1980s, it had been transferred to people who were annoying, and in the modern century it is used as an exclamation in mildly upsetting situations. A hammer on an exposed finger merits the full 'Fuck!'; missing a bus when there's another one due in two minutes might deserve a token 'Fuck-dust!'.

FUCKEE: Someone who is being fucked, not necessarily in a sexual context.

FUCKERWARE: At a Tupperware party, the aim is to persuade gullible housewives to purchase household goods that they don't need by disguising the sales pitch as a social occasion. With Fuckerware, the principle can be the same, only the clients are being offered sex toys. Be wary of accepting an invitation to a

Fuckerware party unless you know your host very well, however: the phrase is also applied to a swingers' gathering where men and women gather to experiment with a box of sex toys and partners who are not their own.

FUCKERY: The nineteenth-century term for a brothel has mutated in recent decades into a description of any kind of nonsense – no sexual activity required. It is used especially in state or corporate attempts to mess with our minds and our daily lives. Remember that the next time you're on the phone to a call centre.

FUCK-EYE: If you give someone the 'fuck-eye', you're employing what used to be called, in more romantic times, a 'come-hither stare'. If your 'fuck-eye' looks like your FUCKFACE, you probably won't be getting any.

FUCKFACE: The gurning expressions pulled by every man and woman when they're experiencing an orgasm. If there's no gurning, they ain't feeling it. Similar expressions can be achieved by other means, such as plunging into hot or cold water, punching someone in sensitive places, or pretty much every activity seen in the *Jackass* film series.

FUCK-FEATURES: Abusive, of course, and pretty much guaranteed not to get someone into bed if you try to attract their attention this way. It suggests ugliness, presumably because someone looks as if they've become stuck in their FUCKFACE.

FUCK-FEST: A glorious cavalcade of sex, which can involve as many people as you like. Sounds more fun than a FUCKATHON, doesn't it?

FUCK FILM: A film in which fucking occurs, usually in a more explicit fashion than you'll see in your local multiplex. Also known as a FUCK-FLICK.

FUCKFINGER: From the nineteenth century, this describes someone who was able to pleasure themselves with their own fingers: also known as a FUCKFIST. Not to be confused with the noun FINGERFUCK, which usually involves more than one person.

FUCK-FLAPS: Another way of saying 'cunt-flaps'. Which is another way of revealing that you're a young man who probably isn't ever going to get anywhere near anyone's labia.

FUCKHEAD: This isn't a sexual practice, but a description of someone who's such an idiot that he (and it usually is a 'he') isn't going to find a girlfriend.

FUCKING MACHINE: Someone who is a great lover – a stud (if it's a man). Or the habitual cry of anyone trying to use a computer, an automatic check-in at the airport, a ticket dispenser, a DVD player, a coffee-maker . . .

FUCKHOLE: The place where . . . look, you're going to have to work this one out for yourselves. First used in the Victorian era. And you thought they were all too busy covering up the legs of tables in case impressionable youngsters became over-excited. Like almost every other sexual term in the twenty-first century, this has been transformed into a term of abuse aimed at young women. The worldwide web has a lot to answer for.

FUCK-IN: We can thank American cartoonist Robert Crumb for this term, first identified in his 1968 illustration of the 'Grand Opening of the Great Intercontinental Fuck-in & Orgy-Riot' (published in the underground mag *Snatch Comics*). See FUCK-FEST.

FUCK-IN-A-FOG: Chroniclers of English slang would have us believe that gardeners with foul minds use this term to describe the fennel flower – or, more poetically, 'love-in-a-mist'. Do not use this in any garden owned by the National Trust.

FUCK-IN-LAW: Someone who becomes related to you via sex. So if I have sex with your sister . . . No, of *course* I haven't had sex with your sister. Honestly. I don't know why I even *mentioned* your sister. I don't find her attractive. No, I'm not saying there's anything wrong with her, she's a lovely girl. Not in that way, obviously. I told you, I don't want to go to bed with her. All right, be like that, leave. I can always phone your sister. What? It was a *joke*. I don't even have her number. I can get it from your mum. No, I *haven't* had sex with your mum, honestly . . .

FUCKJOB: Something that is well and truly 'fucked up'; and therefore also the means by which Person A 'fucks up' Person B, who may or may not deserve it. In the era of internet porn, almost anything sexual is a 'fuckjob', and probably just as mechanical as that term suggests.

FUCK-KNUCKLE: Our Australian cousins get the credit for this mild alternative to the more abusive FUCKHEAD – the gentle nature of the insult presumably conveyed by the fact that the finger is only involved as far as the knuckle.

FUCKLESS WONDER: Someone who's a 'chinless wonder' is posh and stupid (remember Tim Nice-but-Dim?). Someone who's a 'brainless wonder' doesn't have to be posh. And someone who's a 'fuckless wonder' doesn't even have to have a brain.

FUCKLOAD: Used in the phrase 'a fuckload of' on occasions when the more common word 'shitload' simply doesn't capture the moment.

FUCK-ME'S: American gay slang for a tight pair of trousers, though I would have thought that if they were too tight, they might restrict the blood-flow to vital organs.

FUCKMOBILE: A car which the owner believes will enable him to procure a sexual partner; and also the venue for what happens when he does. This only works with certain cars, and certain sexual partners, despite what Jeremy Clarkson might think.

FUCK-MUSCLE: As anyone will know who took biology in school past the point where they make you cut up rats, there is no bone in the human penis – despite the slang word 'boner' for an erection. But there is muscle, though it's not the kind of muscle that you can make grow by exercise, otherwise teenage boys would be even more active in private than they already are. The growth is all about blood, so anyone tempted to use the word 'fuck-muscle' should actually be prepared to accompany it with an anatomical explanation.

FUCK-NEST: See FUCKPAD, but cosier.

FUCKNOB: Slang term for sexual intercourse meets slang word for penis: inevitable consequence is a term of abuse.

FUCKNUT(S): See FUCKNOB, but replace 'penis' with 'testicles' (easier than it sounds). However, someone who is FUCK-NUTTY is also a FUCKAHOLIC: nobody said that the penis didn't have a mind of its own.

FUCKOLA: Sounds as if it should be an X-rated slot machine, but it's actually a right royal cock-up, and not in a good way.

FUCK PAD: You're imagining something unpleasantly intimate that might be hiding in a potential partner's undies, aren't you? It's OK: the person with the fuck pad is merely a throwback to the 1970s, when the pad was where the dude hung out, and where he took his lovely lady with luurve on his mind.

FUCKPLUG: A contraceptive device that seals up the FUCKHOLE to prevent pregnancy. Not recommended for use at intimate moments (the word, that is).

FUCKPOLE: A straight-to-the-point, don't-beat-about-the-bush term for the penis at its most extended. Incidentally, men don't like being told they have a 'fuckpin'.

FUCK-PUMP: No, I don't know where you can buy one . . . for the simple reason that this term is applied to a married man by those who are unfortunate enough not to have a regular sexual partner.

FUCKRIES: A West Indian term – spoken more than written, I'd wager – to describe troubles that are disturbing someone's mental equilibrium.

FUCK-RUBBER: The male equivalent of a FUCK-PLUG.

Extensions

FUCK-SAUCE: The substance that is captured within the FUCK-RUBBER, or has its progress halted by a FUCK-PLUG. If you need any more help, it comes out of a FUCK-STICK when a peak of excitement is reached.

FUCK-SHOW: What you hope you're going to see when you go behind the curtains in a Soho establishment. What you actually get, I'm told, is a bar bill that would pay off the national debt.

FUCK-SOCK: Another charming term for a FUCK-RUBBER – or, for the solo performer, a handy item into which FUCK-SAUCE can be directed to avoid staining the bedclothes.

FUCKSTICK: They say that men don't take kindly to criticism of their performance behind the wheel or in bed. So the ideal compliment for a *Top Gear* kind of guy is to tell him that he handles his gearstick the way he handles his fuckstick; or vice versa, depending which one he shows you first. NB: If someone uses this word in the plural, it doesn't mean that he is a freak of nature, or that she has more than one man in hand; it's merely a twenty-first-century expression of slight annoyance.

FUCKSTRUCK: The state of mind you enjoy when you first establish a sexual relationship, i.e. before you get pregnant, pick up a sexually transmitted disease, or meet the in-laws.

FUCKTRUCK: Certain members of the Australian population drive around in vans just large enough to hold a mattress in the back – flat on the floor, of course. They will then invite lonely souls to join them there for polite conversation. Also known as a 'passion wagon'.

FUCK-UDDERS: A term for 'breasts' used by young men who have only a very confused grasp of the mechanics of human reproduction.

FUCKWAD: A small town between FUCKHEAD and FUCKWIT.

FUCKWIT: A gentler way of saying FUCKHEAD. But not so gentle that you should try it out on the boss.

FUCKY-FUCKY (or FUCK-FUCK): America's involvement in Vietnam during the 1960s and 1970s was not one of the more glorious moments in the nation's history. But, say what you will about the political and military consequences, it did at least enlarge our language, and that of the unfortunate prostitutes who had to service US servicemen on their days off from bombing peasants and being shot at by the Cong. Being quick learners, the young-women-for-hire of Saigon quickly learned to offer 'fucky-fucky' or 'fucky-sucky' to their clients; and the phrase soon made its way back to America, where 'fucky-sucky' on a brothel menu means exactly what it says.

HONEYFUCK: A sexual encounter in the United States that incorporates slightly more romance than one might have expected. Or one that involves a woman somewhat younger than her male partner: Michael Douglas and his lovely Welsh bride, perhaps.

MINDFUCK: Anything that amazes or boggles the brain; and therefore, by extension, a process whereby a person is subjected to a form of brainwashing. Such as reading a book in which the word 'fuck' appears several hundred times.

Extensions

Is This the Way to Timbuktu?

It does not take a massive leap of the imagination to conclude that when you combine the words 'bum' and 'fuck', you arrive at 'bumfuck' – a word that can mean exactly what you think it means. If you saw 'bum' and assumed that we were talking about a person who might otherwise be dubbed an 'arsehole', then you'll have calculated that 'bum' + 'fuck' equals an extremely unpleasant 'arse-hole'.

If, however, you took 'bum' as a 'noun' and 'fuck' as an activity, then you know exactly where you're going, and you would have found yourself fully at home in the Old Testament city of Sodom.

Or, finally, you might take 'bum' to be an adjective – substandard, unsatisfactory, as in 'a bum rap' – and decide, with equal accuracy, that 'bumfuck' is an act of sexual congress that was great, darling, honestly, the earth moved for me too, it really did; but at the front of your mind you really wish you'd been in someone else's bed with someone else (not necessarily the same someone, of course).

None of which prepares us for the newest and most obscure usage of that 'bum' and 'fuck' combination: the phrase that merges the two words as one, and then adds a geographical location on the end. Hence we arrive at 'Bumfuck, Africa' or, more commonly, 'Bumfuck, Egypt'. ('Bumfuck, Illinois' works better for me, but as it was the Americans who came up with these things, maybe that was too close to home.)

As a child, I remember being amazed when I discovered that 'Timbuktu' – which adults were always using to describe an impossibly far-flung destination of no redeeming value – was actually a major city in the African nation of Mali. Imagine growing up there, and discovering that the entire Western world believes your hometown is a joke. It's a bit like being born in Essex.

The point is that, in the collective imagination rather than on the map of what we used to call, both patronisingly and racistly, 'The Dark Continent', 'Bumfuck' and 'Timbuktu' are twin towns. The fact that one of them exists and the other (probably) doesn't – not yet, anyway – is an irrelevance. They're both symbols of being so far off the beaten track that there simply isn't a track to beat. So being sent to Bumfuck is even worse than being sent to Coventry, which is almost certainly twinned with Timbuktu.

The Animal (F')Kingdom

Many of God's creatures have found their way into the lexicon of English swearing, from the humble lark to the mighty . . . well, duck.

BEARS: There is a Canadian TV series that you may have missed, entitled *Trailer Park Boys*: it's the kind of thing that Chris Lilley of *Summer Heights High* fame might have dreamed up if he came from Nova Scotia and couldn't afford a tripod for his camera. And in this series a new phrase was added to the language: 'fucked by bears'. Besides its literal meaning, and the related sense of being attacked by our ursine cousins, it also carries wider connotations, as the worst possible experience that anyone can imagine. Especially if they've spent their entire lives in Nova Scotia.

CAT: Let's leave the poor 'pussy', in all its permutations, out of this, OK? Suffice to say here that if you 'fuck up someone's pussy', you are not necessarily having sexual intercourse (though you might be). A polite translation of this phrase might be 'winding up a rival', and interfering with their cat might hit the spot perfectly. If someone does that to you, you might scream 'Fuck a cat!' in frustration.

CHIMP: For some reason, cartoonists around the world often portrayed President George 'Dubya' Bush as a chimp. So you can probably guess the prime target of the casual insult, 'fuck-chimp', which doesn't mean that he's good in bed. It simply denotes somebody who is hopelessly out of his depth.

COW: A dictionary of casual sexism would be bigger than the Bible and more depressing than the latest list of bankers' bonuses. With the innocent cow already figuring in countless insults aimed at women, it's not surprising that, by extension, it has also been dragged into describing parts of the female anatomy. The result – a triumph of the same refined twenty-first-century imagination that brought you the Kardashian family – is the word 'fuck udders', as a way of describing a pair of breasts. The intelligence of the person who coined this addition to our lustrous language is demonstrated by the fundamental non sequitur at its heart. I can understand (though not condone) a young man who has no female friends describing breasts (as they sometimes do) as 'fuck handles'. And I can see (but not etc etc) the link between breasts and udders: keeping the species alive, and all that. But 'fuck udders' suggests that someone needs some very basic sex education lessons.

DOG: 'Fucking the dog' is military slang for anything that seems like a complete waste of time (everything except fighting and drinking, in other words). A soldier could feel that he is 'fucking the dog' when the sergeant-major tells him to 'paint that fence white, and then paint it black'. By association, the gallant infantryman may choose to 'fuck the dog' by engaging in something that is utterly pointless but looks useful (such as painting the fence), to avoid being commandeered for something less pleasant (e.g. cleaning out the latrines). It is probably best not to imagine what kind of bitter experience led to the original coining of this phrase, which apparently originated during the First World War in a more genteel variant, 'walking the dog'. Or you might prefer to 'fornicate the poodle' (other breeds are also available). Some sources transfer the blame from the dog to the duck, incidentally, and offer a more polite alternative: 'stroke the duck'.

The abbreviation FTD, which probably ought to stand for 'fuckingly transmitted disease', is sometimes used by members of the military to summarise the pointlessness of their duties (see above). But there's also an extended version of the phrase, which commands the lowly private to 'fuck the dog and sell the pups'. What began as an expression of the meaninglessness of army existence has slowly crossed into civilian life, to the point where a young man might lust vainly over a celebrity on the internet, and boast to his equally retarded friends that he would be delighted to have the opportunity to impregnate her and then dispose of her babies. Not recommended as a chat-up line, though.

More recently, young Americans have transferred the humble 'dog-fuck' from sexual braggadocio to non-related aspects of everyday life, as a synonym for trouble – 'deep doo-doo' or 'deep shit', in other words. And, of course, two sexual practices that can often be one and the same – entry from the rear and anal intercourse – have often been decorated with the 'dog-fuck' description, otherwise known as 'doggy-fuck' or 'doggie-fuck' – or, more traditionally, 'doing it doggy style'.

Inevitably, there is also a 'fuckdog' on the prowl: yet another of the marvellously inventive ways invented by young men to describe a young woman of their acquaintance who might actually enjoy having sex. But it can also be applied the other way around, you'll be amazed to hear. If you'd been in Portland, Oregon in 2001, incidentally, you could have witnessed a theatrical production of something called *Poona the Fuckdog*. I'm waiting till it hits Broadway. Those with a musical bent can check out the 1995 album by metal band Autopsy. It's called *Shitfun*, contains tracks called 'Bowel Ripper' and 'I Sodomize Your Corpse', but is worthy of mention here for the 42-second song, 'Fuckdog'.

If someone tells you that they've just fucked a dog in the river, don't look for their water wings: they simply mean they've hidden something (probably deeply illegal) where it will not be found.

DONKEY: Not noted for their intelligence, donkeys are the ideal way to signal your complete ignorance, suggesting that you've blundered your way through something without a clue – as in the phrase, 'I had to fuck a donkey in that meeting'. No asses were harmed in the course of this discussion.

DUCK: Quite how the harmless duck found itself the target of the exasperated exclamation 'Fuck a duck' is a mystery to historians of Britain's verbal curiosities – though the internal rhyming scheme certainly didn't hurt. Its first appearance in print was apparently in the expletive-soaked pages of Henry Miller's *Tropic of Cancer*. More recently it's inspired entire phrases, such as 'Fuck a duck and see what hatches' and 'Fuck a duck and give it a buck'. Linguistic experts claim that the original inspiration was the word 'duckfucker', the person on board a transatlantic ship who was charged with keeping the domestic animals alive, rather than pleasuring them in exotic ways. This word in turn entered American stoner slang as a term for an annoying idiot.

As the award-winning Italian film *Padre Padrone* demonstrated all too graphically, young men in remote country districts have been known to explore their budding sexual urges with the help of a handily placed chicken. But ducks probably flap about too much to make that a satisfying liaison.

Two examples of Cockney rhyming slang might also be worth a quack at this point: Donald Duck, and goose & duck. You can probably work out what they rhyme with. The simple joy of creating a rhythm explains the American phrase 'fucked duck', which is basically anyone – any species, in fact – which is doomed for destruction. Sounds like an ideal slogan for the Green Party.

You might say 'I'll fuck a dead duck!' on occasions when 'Blow me down with a feather' simply doesn't capture the full extent of your surprise. Being told to 'Go fuck a duck' (or a dog, for that matter) is an impolite way of being sent to hell, presumably coined by someone who has actually experimented with trans-species congress. If you are a 'fuck duck', you either have sex regularly with your friends or with people who aren't your friends. And finally, if someone says that you 'fuck a duck', they are suggesting that perhaps you might be spreading your favours too widely. Unless, of course, you really are hanging out too much at your local duck pond.

GOAT: Goats are altogether too frisky to be fucked in the 'sheep' sense (see below). Indeed, the result would almost certainly be chaotic (not to mention downright dangerous for both man and goat). So a 'goat fuck', thanks to our GI buddies, stationed in Britain during the Second World War, is a situation that has got rather out of hand, and is unlikely to reach a positive conclusion. When they're not dragging goats into the fray, American soldiers have been known to call this a 'Chinese fire drill', bringing the planet's most populous nation into the target area. The Chinese phrase for the same cock-up is probably 'American election'.

For entertaining use of the abusive phrase 'Go fuck a goat!', listen out for Mooj's appearance in the 2005 movie, *The 40 Year Old Virgin*.

HORSE: My introduction to the internet, in the days when it took about twenty minutes for the dial-up connection to take hold, and another hour or two for each page to download, involved my selecting something entirely harmless in what passed for a search engine in 1997, pushing 'Enter' – and being rewarded with what we would now call a 'gif' of a woman and a horse getting to know each other in a surprisingly intimate way. After which I was not at all surprised to hear that horses were being dragged into the arena of sexual innuendo, with young men boasting that they had 'fucked a horse', not in the Biblical sense, but as an expression of whole-hearted enjoyment of their climax. The saucier the filly, the better.

LARK: 'Fuck this for a lark,' people used to say when they were faced with something too tedious to deserve their attention. That was, of course, a lark in the sense of a frolic, a game, a jolly good time, rather than the garden bird otherwise known as the skylark. None of which prevented Sir Laurence Olivier, no less, from adopting a very literal, bird-centred French translation of the phrase during his stewardship of the National Theatre: 'Baisez cela pour une alouette'.

LIZARD: Specifically, the 'fuck-you lizard', as American servicemen during the Vietnam War named the tokay gecko – simply and sensibly because the amphibian's natural call sounded (to stoned American ears) like 'fuck you'.

MINK: Some teenage girls refer to their private parts as their 'minky'. This may or may not be relevant to the phrase 'fuck like a mink', which has traditionally been used to refer to women but not men (see Rattlesnake below). Minks are small, furry creatures that are notoriously promiscuous and unwilling to form lasting sexual relationships. They mate violently, with the male often seizing the nape of the female's neck with his teeth, while holding her down with his paws. Any similarity to the scene outside an English seaside tavern on a Friday night is purely coincidental.

MONKEY: Bored with saying 'fuck a duck'? 'Fuck a monkey' will work equally well as a demonstration of your verbal dexterity. No doubt other animals could be brought into the cage as well, but be careful of the ones with claws.

MOOSE: 'Fuck a moose' is probably only an appropriate exclamation for Canadians. But that hasn't prevented death metal band Flesh Parade incorporating the phrase into a track ('Eat Shit and Fuck a Moose') that sounds as if it was recorded just after the singer was set on fire.

PIG: Pigs have curly tails (and penises, but let's not go there). And that, by a complex process of association and translation down the centuries, is why we have the word 'screw' (a means of fixing two objects together, that is). The derivation goes like this: from the Latin word for 'sow' (*scrofa*) to the medieval French (*escroue*) and then into English, once the man-of-war ferry service from Calais to Dover had opened in 1539 (I'm sure I read that on Wikipedia).

Anyway: 'fuck-pig' (Cockney in origin) is an insult, suggesting that someone is so filthy that they might actually do what the phrase suggests; and so is 'pigfucker' – the latter representing a more contemptuous variant on the better-known 'sheep-shagger'. For a literary rendering, try Brendan Behan's invention in his 1958 play *Borstal Boy*: 'fugh-pig', the first syllable definitely not rhyming with 'hugh'.

RABBIT: The one thing everyone knows about rabbits is that they have babies. Lots of babies. So presumably they must have sex somewhere along the line. Someone who 'fucks like a rabbit' – or like a bunny – could therefore be said to have a voracious appetite for sex (rather than a lot of babies). A 'fuck bunny', meanwhile, is someone who likes being serviced by someone who 'fucks like a bunny', especially if she (usually) looks as if she's as sweet as pie.

RAT: Nobody likes to boast that they fuck like a rat (or a mouse, for that matter). So 'ratfuck' is, you'll be amazed to learn, not a compliment. In American criminal circles, a 'fink' was an informer or stool pigeon; a particularly egregious example of the species was given the intensified label of 'ratfink'. When American cartoonist Ed Roth invented a hot-rod character named 'Rat Fink' in the early 1960s, the insult lost much of its power. Instead, members of the underworld retained the 'rat', dropped the 'fink', and substituted a different four-letter word ending in a 'k'. The resulting word was every bit as damning of an associate's character as 'ratfink' had once been. By extension, 'ratfuck' also came to mean someone who was utilising political 'dirty tricks' – fucking someone up like a dirty rat, in other words.

It enjoyed particular popularity during Richard 'Tricky Dicky' Nixon's 1972 presidential re-election campaign (which incidentally used the stunningly appropriate acronym, CREEP).

But it was not one of the multitude of four-letter words captured on tape in President Nixon's office, and subsequently disclosed to the committee investigating the Watergate scandal. Nixon always preferred a simple 'fuck' with no frills.

RATTLESNAKE: While women are compared to minks, men are sometimes said in America (and Australia, where there are no rattlesnakes outside zoos) to 'fuck like a rattlesnake'. Barry Humphries incorporated the phrase into one of his Barry McKenzie cartoon strips in the late Sixties.

The more you learn about the mating habits of the rattlesnake, the less complimentary the phrase sounds. Male rattlesnakes single out a prospective sexual partner, then trail round after her for days, refusing to take 'no' for an answer. They continually touch her in inappropriate places, in a vain attempt to arouse her. If another male gets in the way, they wind their bodies around each other and sprawl on the ground until one of them gives in. After that, coupling takes the form of a series of uncoordinated spasms. Many women readers may feel a tinge of recognition at this point. Someone who 'fucks like a rattlesnake' will also 'go like the clappers'.

RHINO: Another recent invention: 'fuck a rhino' as a suggestion to a friend (the 'go' at the start of the phrase is both invisible and silent).

SHEEP: Sheep-fuckers, or more commonly sheep-shaggers, are local yokels so simple and desperate that they'll couple with anything soft, warm and slow on the uptake – all of which makes the none-too-bright sheep an easy target. The English use the phrase to insult the Welsh, the Aussies to ridicule their cousins in New Zealand, and so on and on. Anybody who owns a sheep is likely to hear this phrase at least once in their lives, regardless of how intimate they are with their flock.

SPIDER: Students of the English language who dedicated themselves to research in the more dubious districts of Singapore claim to have heard the exasperated exclamation: 'Fuck spider!'. However, given the viciousness of some arachnids in those parts, what they may actually have heard is 'Fuck! Spider!'. If you happen to be in Singapore, asking an attractive young person for a date, and they tell you to 'Go fuck spider', you should think about putting an ad in the Lonely Hearts column instead.

You Can Leave Your Shoes On

Fuck-me pumps. Fuck-me shoes. Fuck-me boots. Or, if you prefer, come-fuck-me pumps. Or catch-me-and-fuck-me shoes.

The common denominator? Joan Crawford. She was hardly the first – or, in her time, the only – actress to accentuate her height, her *hauteur* or indeed her sexual appeal by donning a pair of cross-laced high heels. Such footwear has become a signifier of alluring female beauty around the world, despite the fact that these shoes are (a) usually painful to wear, (b) apparently designed to leave the feet looking as if they've been used as a garden implement and (c) constructed in such a way as to make it impossible – or embarrassingly ridiculous – for the wearer to walk. (Women in catch-me-and-fuck-me shoes therefore aren't actually that difficult to catch, which may be the point.) But what are comfort, safety, and dignity when you can perch perilously atop a pair of six-inch wedges?

I digress. We were talking about Joan Crawford, whose tempestuous career involved success, failure, success, failure (you get the idea), notoriety, and an alleged propensity to apply her coat-hanger to sensitive areas of her children's behinds. A star from the Thirties onwards, she was by the end of her movie career established not just as a Hollywood legend, but as an icon for the increasingly vocal section of the gay community who identified themselves with flamboyant and troubled divas from the worlds of stage and screen. None of these particular admirers would have been likely to feel any great sexual desire for Ms Crawford, but that didn't prevent them from worshipping her erotic image and (for those who felt that way inclined) echoing her appearance in their own trans-gender clothing expeditions.

By the early Seventies, the phrase 'fuck-me pumps' had been coined (by Americans, naturally, as nobody in Britain talked about pumps forty years ago), and was sometimes linked, in conversation and then in print, with Joan Crawford. Once established, the link became unbreakable, as if her 'fuck-me pumps' had been on the lips of everyone in the Hollywood community. And so her expansive career in the flicks has been reduced to a casual reference to her shoes, and a folk memory of the movie *Mommie Dearest*, based on her daughter's exposé of her mother's disciplinary habits.

David Bowie, no stranger himself to Crawford-style dress or demeanour, can be given credit for introducing the phrase 'fuck-me pumps' into popular culture at large – or at least he could have been, had the phrase been more distinguishable among the garbled, cut-up images of his 1974 recording 'We Are the Dead'. Thirty years later, 'Fuck Me Pumps' was one of the songs on Amy Winehouse's debut album, *Frank*, though she only uttered the dreaded word at the very end of the recording, her first rendering of the phrase restricting itself to 'f me pumps'. (The song was coyly listed as 'F**k Me Pumps' on the back of the CD, although the booklet inside bravely printed the title in full.)

But for the British chattering classes, both these references have paled into insignificance alongside a printed reference to 'fuck-me shoes'. It originated in a newspaper spat between two columnists from different generations, each of a firmly feminist bent, but each reserving the right to carve her own idiosyncratic path through the jungle of political correctness. Germaine Greer was a controversialist with nearly three decades of experience by the time she clashed with Suzanne Moore, a relative neophyte by comparison. They fell out, ostensibly, over Moore's references in a newspaper to Greer's sexual and gynaecological history; and in reply, Greer painted an acerbic verbal portrait of her antagonist, castigating Moore in a rather unfeminist fashion for her 'hair birds-nested all over the place, fuck-me shoes and three fat layers of cleavage'. *The Guardian*, which hosted columns by both women, refused to print this submission, provoking Greer into leaving the paper in high dudgeon, though she seems to have recovered her equilibrium; while Moore, she of the offending heels, continued to respect Greer both as a feminist pioneer and a challenging thinker while suggesting politely that it might have been better if she had been criticised for what came out of her mouth rather than what went onto her feet. Greer's comments circulated amongst the cognoscenti, in any case, ensuring that the reliably thought-provoking Moore is likely to be pursued to her grave by the memory of her 'fuck-me shoes'. And – sorry, Suzanne – this account probably hasn't helped.

Catch Me If You Can

'Catch-me-and-fuck-me' doesn't only refer to shoes. It's been applied to a number of fashion items that either suggest sexual allure or (warning: irony ahead) lack of it. In particular, pieces of equipment issued to American service personnel tend to qualify: catch-me-fuck-me shorts because they're so damn short, catch-me-fuck-me goggles because they're so damn ugly. And in Australia, 'catch me fuck me' is a national sport, and not in the way you might think: it's a slang term for the only-men-need-apply game of Rugby League. Gives a whole new meaning to the 'up and under' that old Eddie Waring was always talking about, doesn't it?

Say What?

An Alien's Guide to Simple British Phrases

AWA' TAE FUCK: 'I beg to differ', but only in Scotland.

FUCKED TO A FARE-THEE-WELL: 'I seem to be in deep doo-doo.'

FUCK ME AND THE BABY'S YOURS: Guaranteed chat-up line for a one-night stand.

FUCK ME BACKWARDS: 'I could only be more surprised if you did, in fact, fuck me backwards.'

FUCK ME GENTLY WITH A CHAINSAW: 'I am having trouble believing what you are telling me.'

FUCK ME HARDER: 'Why don't you say something even more annoying?'

FUCK ME RAGGED: 'I am in a slight state of shock.'

FUCK ME SIDEWAYS: 'I am coming to realise that my view of the world was slightly naïve.'

FUCK MY DAYS: 'Gosh, how annoying.'

FUCK MY LUCK: 'Would you believe it?'

FUCK MY OLD BOOTS: 'You could have blown me down with a feather.'

FUCK THAT FOR A GAME OF SOLDIERS: Or a top hat, or a game of skittles, or a comic song, or a laugh, or a month in Southend.

FUCK THE BEGRUDGERS: 'Golly gosh. Did I mention that I'm from Ireland?'

FUCK THE WORLD: 'I am not a good bet for a stable marriage.'

FUCK YOU, CHARLIE: Or, more softly, Chuck You, Farley.

FUCK YOU JACK: Sequel to the Peter Sellers film *I'm All Right, Jack*.

FUCK YOU VERY MUCH: 'Thanks. But no thanks.'

FULL OF FUCK: Beginning to feel slightly randy.

GET THE FUCK OUT: 'Please leave immediately.'

GET TO FUCK: 'Are you quite sure about that?'

HE'D FUCK ANYTHING WITH A HOLE IN IT: 'His eyesight is not what it was.'

INTERNATIONAL FUCK-YOUR-BUDDY WEEK: Time to blame your colleagues for your mistakes.

I WOULDN'T FUCK HER WITH A BORROWED PRICK: 'I find her company slightly distasteful.'

TAKE A FLYING FUCK AT A RUBBER DUCK: Or a rolling doughnut, as you prefer. In either case, please bugger off.

THROW A FUCK INTO SOMEONE: A poetic way of saying 'fuck'.

TO BE FUCKED IN THE CAR: To suffer the slings and arrows of outrageous fortune, but only in Canada.

TO FUCK THAT INTO A COCKED HAT: Outdo the opposition.

TO GO LIKE THE HAMMERS OF FUCK: To be energetic.

TO GO ON THE FUCK: Become a prostitute.

WHO DO I HAVE TO FUCK TO GET OFF THIS PICTURE?: The casting couch in reverse.

YOU CAN FUCK ME BUT YOU CAN'T MAKE ME LIKE THE BABY: 'I probably don't fancy you, but I've had so much to drink that I'm prepared to give you bed-room, just this once.'

Excursions

The Famous Austrian Sense of Humour

The British sense of humour is notoriously childish, veering at best to the adolescent. So it is not a surprise that, to our eyes, the funniest place in the whole wide world is the tiny Austrian village of . . . (wait for it) . . . Fucking.

Yes, Fucking.

I know. Isn't that hysterical?

OK, we've got that out of our system.

Actually, we haven't.

Right.

This time I think I can hold it together (just like they do in Fucking) . . .

Now I'm being serious. Fucking – no, not amusing at all – is on the road from Tarsdorf to Haid, which also passes through the village of Hucking. And it's near the equally insignificant hamlets of Wupping and Wolfing, which sound rather like another way of saying . . . no, that's not funny.

And the name of the road that links Hucking and Fucking is, of course . . . Fuckinger Strasse. Which, if you ever get bored, means that you go onto Google Maps, put in Fucking, Austria as your target, and you can find about a dozen roads, all marked with the word 'Fucking' on them . . . hang on a minute: they've changed it! Now it says 'Hucking' all over the map. Curses! Someone must have noticed. That's not nearly as funny.

Anyway, there are bus stops, apparently, at two places in Fucking: Unterfucking and Oberfucking (Lower Fucking and Upper Fucking to you). And the strange thing is that there is *another* Unterfucking in Austria, very close to the German border. And, a few feet away, another Oberfucking as well. But there's no Fucking there, I can promise you.

Back to Fucking, as the actress . . . no, I must stop that. Nobody in Fucking thinks that the Fucking name is remotely hilarious. In fact, they are heartily sick of anyone who speaks English coming anywhere near them. They are especially tired of journalists from Britain or America phoning them for comments, which is probably why journalists from Britain or America run pretty much exactly the same story about Fucking every three or four years. Each time, there's a new Fucking mayor to talk to, but the mayor always says the same thing: 'Leave Fucking alone! We don't want to talk about Fucking. Fucking is nothing to do with you.' Or as the police commissioner supposedly told the *Daily Telegraph* back in 2005 (when it was just as funny as it is now): 'It may be very amusing for you British, but Fucking is simply Fucking to us. What is this big Fucking joke? It is puerile.' And I can't disagree with that. Funny, though, isn't it?

What problems have been caused by this interest in Fucking? Well, the street signs keep being stolen, even when they're erected in steel and laid in concrete. And if they haven't been stolen, then tourists stand in front of them, usually without their clothes, so they can send photos of themselves stark bollock naked in a Fucking street beside the Fucking sign.

And then there are the phone calls, aimed randomly at one of the one hundred or so Fucking inhabitants. This is how it normally goes down:

(*ring ring*)

'Ja? Hello?'

'Hi. I want Fucking.'

'Ja, you have come to the right place.'

'You are Fucking?'

'Ja, this is Fucking!'

Yet despite this, as a Fucking planning official once said, 'We are proud of our beautiful Fucking.' A handful of locals have even been selling commemorative Fucking goods, such as Fucking pencils and Fucking postcards. In 2012, though, there was a Fucking shock, when some of the Fucking people tried to get the name of their town changed to . . . Fugging.

Sadly for them, but happily for us, there was already another Fugging town a couple of hundred kilometres away, and regional officials didn't want any confusion between Fucking and Fugging. So the two villages will have to stay exactly as they are, one Fucking and one Fugging. But both adding greatly to the collective joy of the human race – or at least the important part that speaks English.

Welcome to the House of . . .

It's a charming slogan, 'Zum Glück giht's Fück', and indeed with good fortune you may find the House of Fuck – or, as the owners would prefer it to be known, Haus Fück. This is not a sex shop, or a house of shame, but a thoroughly respectable establishment which 'offers over 100 years of typical authentic family hospitality' (though not all at once).

Yes, the Haus Fück is a hotel in the German town of Leverkusen, the home of the Bayer football team, a phenomenally huge illuminated advertising sign for the chemical company that gave the club its name – and a hotel with, for English-speaking visitors at least, a slightly unfortunate title.

It's true that the 'u' in Fück carries an all-important umlaut above it, which alters its pronunciation in a crucial fashion and also explains the hotel's rather disappointing website address: www.hotel-fueck.de. But the British have never liked to concern themselves too much with the finer points of foreign languages, so for our purposes the Haus Fück is still the overnight location with the most enticing title the other side of London's Beaver Hotel. 'Our guests and friends are travellers from around the world,' the establishment boasts, and I'd wager that a fair percentage of them are juvenile-minded Brits, Americans, Canadians and Australians (we'll let the New Zealanders off) anxious to tweet a photo of themselves in front of the hotel sign.

So, while we're poking fun at perfectly innocent continentals, we should note that the hotel translates its advertising slogan as 'Luckily there is Fück', and invites guests to 'Ask us about specials', including 'group rates' for the friends who want to get much friendlier. But remember, all those of you with *very* special-ised tastes: pets are 'only allowed after enquiry', so make sure that your sheep has got its story straight if you're travelling in mixed company. The Brasserie promises 'a spectacular end to the day', while the more modest guests can 'celebrate undis-turbed' in the Club Room. But watch out for the restaurant, with its 'moody atmosphere' – not recommended if your marriage is already on the rocks. And don't worry if you usually have to reserve a single room: 'For individual requirements we are at your disposal'. And they don't offer that at the Beaver Hotel.

Prost!

The vast majority of young Germans now speak our language better than the English do, and can probably swear in several other European tongues as well. So it's not surprising that businesses in Deutschland have now begun to exploit and celebrate the innocent appearance of the F-word in their own vocabulary, as well as offering the thrill of the forbidden to anyone who shares their mastery of Anglo-American obscenity.

Sadly, none of that was sufficient to save the proprietors of Fucking Good Concerts, a promoter in Stuttgart, from ceasing operations a few years back. But another much larger company has survived and indeed prospered as a distributor of clothing, footwear, soft drinks, and a variety of alcoholic beverages. Now, Germany already had a Bavarian brand of beer invitingly called Hell (which surely begged for the existentialist marketing slogan, 'Hell is other beers'). But was the nation ready for Fucking Hell beer from the Fucking Hell company of Berlin?

Not quite, it transpired. None of their young customers batted an F-word eyelid, or baulked at putting on a Fucking Hell T-shirt for the morning after the night before. But somebody with a more grown-up view of the world and absolutely no sense of humour succeeded in banning Fucking Hell GmbH from operating under that name any longer.

In the great tradition of liberationists everywhere, the Fucking Hell boys and girls were not going to let lawyers and bureaucrats prevent them from flooding Germany with their joyous English brand name, and so they employed their own experts to fight the prohibition all the way into some very obscure business court operated by vastly overpaid lawyers and bureaucrats at the European Commission.

Their verdict? 'The examiner rejected the application that the sign used sexuality in order to express contempt and violent anger . . . the word combination contains no semantic indication that could refer to a certain person or group of persons. Nor does it incite a particular act. It cannot even be understood as an instruction that the reader should go to hell . . . Nor can it be considered as reprehensible to use existing place names [remember the lovely town of Fucking in Austria] in a targeted manner (as a reference to the place), merely because this may have an ambiguous meaning in other languages.'

In other words, it was fine to call your beer Fucking Hell as long as you were in Germany, you weren't in a bad mood, you weren't trying to be sexy or violent, or violently sexy, or sexually violent, and you weren't trying to be funny. Heaven forbid.

Commercial Break

You know, maybe including the F-word in your business identity isn't so smart a move after all. Fuckingrats is/was a 'Creative Web Developers Corporation' in Argentina, which landed at least one contract in Britain, for the 2009 Festival of the Moving Image at the University of London. A few months later, they were boasting that they had just completed a new Facebook app for a sex shop in Houston, Texas, but since then their web profile has slipped from buzzing to damn near non-existent. But should you find yourself in need of a very low-profile web designer in Rosario, Argentina, at least you now know where to turn.

But there is a real success story to report, at least at the time of writing. The two founders of Good Fucking Design Advice offer a variety of merchandise (wallpaper, coffee mugs, T-shirts, etc.) that displays messages that you might want to convey to the world – or, if you're a team leader, to the slackers who yawn and scratch themselves in front of you every morning (between fag breaks). Take your pick from 'Show Some Fucking Passion', 'Believe In Your Fucking Self' and the timeless favourite, 'Work Fucking Harder'.

Goodfuckingdesignadvice.com should be your first port of call, if you can be arsed.

If You Go Down to the Woods Today . . .

'Have Sex, Save the World' is the kind of slogan that should appeal to everyone – well, everyone who isn't married to a smelly man who leaves his socks on when he goes to bed. It's also the ethical basis of a German environmental group whose activities have now spread around the world.

They're called Fuck For Forest – which, coincidentally, is also the title of the 2013 documentary movie devoted to their cause. The initial Fuck For Forest collective was based in Berlin, where a bunch of young, slim, probably vegetarian women and men, who favour piercings and tattoos more than clothes, and who are determined to prevent the planet from experiencing ecological disaster, came together in more ways than one. Their primary product was what they call 'Eco-porn', available only to members who subscribe to their website. 'Sex is often shown to attract us to buy all kinds of bullshit products and ideas,' they say, 'so why not for a good cause?' Their subscribers can view Fuck For Forest's home-made erotica, with all proceeds channelled towards environmental projects in the Third World. So perhaps you should consider signing up for Porn Aid – the most useful fun you can have with your clothes off.

Three Days of Peace, Love and . . .

Holy Fuck, Fuck Buttons, the Fuck Ups, Fuck Dat, the Fuck Off and Dies – sometimes you wonder if these bands might have achieved more if they had put less of their creative energy into raising two fingers to the establishment and more into their music. After their initial teenage thrill of punk-rock self-righteousness, what's left? No airplay, no TV exposure, and a somewhat reduced chance of being asked to appear at their local church hall.

So there must have been much rejoicing among the F-word music community when the first Festival of the Fuck Bands was staged in America in 2000. It allowed this tragically persecuted minority to enjoy a rare moment of kindred spirit, and swap war stories about the discrimination and outrage that has been their lot over the previous twelve months. This irregular F-fest reached its inevitable climax in November 2008, when the Festival of the Fuck Bands found its ideal home – in the Austrian village of Fucking.

As 10,000 Marbles, the lead guitarist of the band Fucked Up, explained after the event, the Festival confirmed one basic fact: 'There is an art form to properly using "fuck" in your band's name. A lot of kids these days just use "fuck" for shock value. I think it properly represents what it is we do on stage. Seeing [the band's frontman] Father Damian take off all his clothes and open a wound on his forehead is, in my opinion, pretty fucked up.' And they say that the golden age of rock'n'roll is dead.

Sadly, since 2008, the Festival of the Fuck Bands seems to have slipped into a coma, perhaps because the participants can't decide where to hold the next one – the Austrian village of Fuckersberg; the German town of Prichsenstadt, where there's a pond called Fuckersee; or Laufersweiler, another German location, where a marquee could perhaps be erected in Fuckerter Weg.

Whilst we're taking childish pleasure in such things, may I draw your attention to the varied delights of such tourist attractions as Dildo in Canada (don't miss the popular Dildo Trading Post), Muff in Northern Ireland (would you believe that there is a Muff Diving Club?), Wank in Germany (only single rooms available), or one of the enticing options available in France: the villages of Pussy, Anus, and Condom. After which you may be ready for a rest cure in the Massachusetts district of Shagged.

Swearing in Europe: A Cautionary Note

No European language (though to be honest I haven't checked whatever it is they speak in Lapland) has a word that equates to every diverse usage of 'fuck' in the English tongue. Indeed, 'fuck' might lay claim to being Europe's most versatile word, though don't quote me on that. (You want statistics, call an accountant.)

What quickly becomes apparent when you talk to natives of other countries is that swearing is an art best acquired through experience – in other words, you really need to be born there. Just as the F-word has subtly different meanings depending on the context, and the tone of voice, the same applies to profanities in foreign languages.

In France, for example, where what we consider to be 'bad language' is never censored on TV, both '*Je m'en fous*' and '*J'en ai rien à foutre*' mean something along the lines of our 'I don't give a fuck'. 'Foutre' equates to the sexual meaning of the F-word; but then so does 'baiser', though the latter can also refer to nothing more graphic than kissing (so use with care, in other words). On the streets of Paris, though, the word most commonly heard from passers-by is 'putain', which literally means 'whore'. It's actually an all-purpose explanation, which works whether you're admiring someone's new haircut or trapping your finger in a car door. Don't shout it at women sheltering from the rain in shop doorways, however, unless you want to hear them shout it back.

German swearing is more inclined to favour bathroom functions over sexuality (something that we Brits, with our 'arse', 'fart', 'turd', 'piss', and 'shit', ought to appreciate). The verb 'ficken' literally means 'to fuck', but it's rarely used as a profanity. You'll more often hear 'Scheisse' (shit), 'Arschloch' (arsehole), or 'Wichser' (wanker) as outbursts than anything directly related to the act of intercourse.

Spanish swearing is complicated by the fact that every area, and every Latin American country that speaks the language, has its own specific swear-words. 'Joder' is a useful 'fuck' verb to remember, though. And depending where you are in Italy, a blast of 'fottiti' or 'vaffanculo' will persuade your listener to go and fuck themselves, if they're so inclined.

Perhaps the most sensible swearers in Europe are the Scandinavians. Though they have plenty of their own rude words, they have gradually assimilated some of ours too. Which is why viewers of *The Killing* have become used to hearing Sarah Lund mutter 'fuck' every time she discovers that another of her sidekicks is actually a serial killer. There you are: I've managed to use the words 'fuck' and 'Sarah Lund' in the same sentence, without saying anything about how strangely, compellingly, devilishly attractive the woman is, especially when she's angry – which is pretty much all the time. You'd be the same if your sidekick was a serial killer.

Baptisms

Kenneth Tynan's TV Burp

In the far-off days of the Sixties, when Mary Whitehouse was prepared to lead her battalion of clean-up TV campaigners into action at the first hint of an innuendo, even the mildest profanity was likely to arouse a storm of press-primed outrage. No one on television upset Mrs Whitehouse's sensitive ears more than Alf Garnett, the authentic voice of middle-aged English prejudice in Johnny Speight's *Till Death Us Do Part*. Yet for all his reputation as the doyen of comic filth, Alf was comparatively restrained in his choice of expletives. While Mary's diligent statisticians calculated the precise number of 'bloodys' and 'damns' in each episode, Alf never let slip the four-letter word that would have been most likely to spew from the lips of a real-life Garnett. Indeed, Andy Murray says the F-word more often in an average tennis match (especially if his first serve isn't working) than Alf did throughout his entire twenty-five-year run on TV.

So it was left to an altogether more educated voice to widen the vocabulary of the Innocent British Public. The Oxford-educated Kenneth Tynan was a renowned theatre critic for the

F**k

Evening Standard, the *New Yorker* and *The Observer*, and – by 1965 – the literary manager, no less, of Laurence Olivier's National Theatre. Though he still preferred to think of himself as the *enfant terrible* of British cultural life, he was 38 years old and at the heart of the establishment.

But he had form when it came to startling the horses (or at least those horses who could read). In 1960, he had persuaded his editor at *The Observer* to allow him to use the word 'fuck' in a commentary on the trial that would determine whether *Lady Chatterley's Lover* was fit for human consumption. Even so, the BBC producers who invited him to appear on the late-night show *BBC-3* in November 1965 must have assumed that he would respect the niceties of the era. *BBC-3* mixed satire and cultural discussion in the tradition of *That Was the Week That Was*, gently lampooning prominent figures and puncturing holes in the British class system. On 13 November, Tynan took part in a high-brow (particularly on the part of the interviewer, Robert 'Combover' Robinson) discussion with American novelist Mary McCarthy about the issue of censorship. In 1965, all British theatrical discussions had to meet the approval of the Lord Chamberlain, who could snip or slash a script without the right of appeal.

Robinson asked Tynan whether he would be willing, if censorship were abolished, to sanction a National Theatre production that featured an act of sexual intercourse. It was the moment Tynan had been waiting for. 'Oh, I think so, certainly,' he drawled in his peculiar, stuttering, slightly contemptuous tone. Then, rather than attempting to tackle Robinson's question, he delivered a line that he had clearly prepared in advance: 'I doubt if there are very many rational people in this world to whom the word "fuck" is particularly diabolical or revolting or totally forbidden'.

It was a calculated stab in the vitals of British censorship and propriety. Even today, most TV presenters would panic, and splutter an apology, to be repeated ad infinitum throughout the remainder of the programme. But Robinson was made of stronger stock, and calmly proceeded with the conversation as if we were all men and women of the world.

There the matter might have rested, if the British outrage industry hadn't geared itself up for maximum production. There were newspaper calls for the BBC to 'Sack 4-Letter Tynan' and cries that he had perpetrated an 'Insult To Womanhood' (men presumably being too worldly to shock). The BBC merely issued an 'expression of regret', while senior executive Hugh Wheldon declared that the subject had been handled 'responsibly, intelligently, and reasonably'.

The House of Commons was dragged into the dispute: four Conservative members tabled motions attacking the BBC; three Labour MPs countered with amendments declaring their support for Tynan and the corporation. Tynan himself issued a statement: 'I used an Old English word in a completely neutral way to illustrate a serious point, just as I would have used it in similar conversation with any group of grown-up people. To have censored myself would, in my view, have been rather an insult to the viewers' intelligence.'

Many members of the public took the issue more seriously, inundating Tynan's post-bag with letters of disgust. (The fact that most of them had not seen the programme, which was broadcast just before midnight, didn't dampen their anger.) Tynan showed his friends one choice example. 'You will soon have the sack,' it trumpeted, 'and my friends and I will be waiting for you, to give you the best licking that you have ever had.' Which, ironically, might have been right up Tynan's street: posthumous publication of his diaries revealed that the theatre critic and professional controversialist was also a keen sado-masochist, who enjoyed nothing more than the prospect of a stiff hand smacking a bare bottom.

It was left to cartoonist Trog, in *The Observer* a week after Tynan's calculated outburst, to apply some British common sense to the affair. He pictured a drinker in a bar, telling his mate: 'I 'ad a few ----ing drinks in the ----ing boozer, then I ----ed off 'ome an' turned on the ----ing telly an' ---- me if Ken ----ing Tynan don't open his ----ing mouth an' come out with this ----ing word for sexual intercourse.'

And Now on Film Four-Letter Word

Shy, retiring creatures that they are, especially in Hollywood, American film-makers were slow to respond to the liberation of the four-letter word in the late Sixties. The Korean War satire *M*A*S*H* (1970) is generally agreed to have been the first mainstream US movie to toss the word around with gay abandon.

In Britain, however, the taboos were stretched a full three years earlier. In December 1967, Michael Winner's *I'll Never Forget Whatshisname* was premiered in London. Marianne Faithfull, already notorious as the girlfriend of Rolling Stones singer Mick Jagger and as 'the naked girl in a rug' at the Stones' 1967 drugs bust, made a two-minute cameo as Oliver Reed's love interest. That was time enough for her to purr her dialogue like a convent girl, strip off, take a bath, and then feature in a kaleidoscopic nightmare. In a voice less like that of a convent girl and more like a psychotic fishwife's, she screams at Reed: 'You fucking bastard, you come out here.' Some of the impact is masked by the blare of a car horn, however, which was added at the request of the British Board of Film Censorship.

Yet Faithfull's 'fucking' trailed in the wake of the front-runner in cinema's four-letter sprint: Joseph Losey's *Ulysses*, first screened in New York in March 1967, and then three months later in

London. The delay was enforced by our old friend the censor, who kicked up such a stink about this movie that audiences flocked to the film, expecting nothing less than some full-bore rumpy-pumpy. They were disappointed: *Ulysses* was simply an honourable attempt to translate the epic all-human-life-in-a-day of James Joyce's novel into two hours of (vaguely) narrative cinema. Its fidelity to the book meant that it had to reflect Molly Bloom's 100-page stream-of-consciousness monologue, during which she (understandably, with 100 pages to fill) occasionally resorted to the shortest and bluntest of foul language. The result was that several 'fucks' made it into the script, alongside some fruity (for 1967) discussion of Leopold Bloom's sexual performance. 'Nyet,' said the censor. Losey replied by snipping out the offending passages – no, not *those* kinds of passage – and replacing them with a blank white screen. He resubmitted the film, whereupon the censor saw the foolishness of his ways and allowed Losey to reinstate all his 'fucks' and 'cocks'. A rare victory for fucking over fucking bureaucrats, you might say.

There was an amusing postscript to this saga. In 1973, the BBC finally plucked up the courage to screen *Ulysses* on TV, although they ensured the minimum number of complaints by scheduling it in the early hours of the morning (well past Mary Whitehouse's bedtime). When the film was over and Molly had uttered her final 'fuck', there was a brief summary of the news. It ended with a snippet about the controversy aroused by a new Rolling Stones song, 'Starfucker'. Convinced that at two in the morning, a *Ulysses*-hardened audience was unlikely to complain, the bulletin not only named the song in question, but proceeded to play its equally graphic chorus in full – its first and last ever BBC broadcast. At which point even Mrs Whitehouse was too exhausted to complain.

F**k

Five Movies That Dare Not Speak Their Name

(1) *FUCK* (1968): Aware that even underground cinemas might
be cautious about screening a film entitled *Fuck*, artist Andy Warhol
revised the title of this epic to *Blue Movie* before its extremely
limited release in 1969. Like his marathon *Sleep* (the ultimate in
insomnia cures), Warhol's *Fuck* lived up to its title, with his 'super-
star' Viva and Louis Waldron devoting thirty minutes of their
two-hour 'fly-on-the-wall' showcase to the act of making love.
Thereafter, they effectively talk about the weather, the blue-tinted
screen the only nod to the promise of the title. It's not even a
particularly erotic encounter. 'We don't want to see your ugly cock
and balls,' Viva complains at one point.

(2) *FUCK* (1999): Premiered at the Museum of Modern Art in Paris,
and shown many years later at Tate Modern, Yves-Marie Mahé's
seven-minute avant-garde video features black-and-white clips of
hardcore pornography, from erection to eruption, interrupted by
flashing visual disturbance and the occasional scrawl of the movie's
title across the screen. Meanwhile, the soundtrack blares industrial
white noise, occasionally giving way to a romantic French pop song.
There are easier ways to get your kicks, believe me.

(3) *FUCK* (2001): They're definitely getting longer . . . though no
easier to swallow. Make way for the full nine minutes of Sean
Gallagher's tale of a baffled Texan called Art. And baffled was the
most generous response to this movie, awarded a special citation
by film fans at the University of Texas for 'cinematic intransigence'.
I think that means they didn't like it.

(4) *FUCK* (2003): William Dickerson's ten-minute drama proves
conclusively that size doesn't matter, as it compresses a lifetime of

70

drama into the time it takes to carry an average woman halfway to orgasm (statistics courtesy of researchers Masters and Johnson). The hero of Dickerson's *Fuck* lies on his hospital bed, recalling significant moments in his life, only to be interrupted when the bleeper on his life-support system suddenly stops. He has time for one last word: 'Fuck'. I'll leave you to guess what happens next.

(5) *FUCK* (2005): This is the king of *Fuck* movies, the only one available on DVD, and the only one you could show to your ageing parents (although you should maybe press the 'mute' button first). It was billed as a 'F*ckumentary film by Steve Anderson', who assembled a montage of interviews, archive clips, folklore and hard fact about the English-speaking world's favourite word. (Strange that nobody's done a book like that.) Among the participants: Hunter S. Thompson, Billy Connolly, Alanis Morissette, and bland Fifties pop star Pat Boone, who reveals that whenever he's aroused to a frenzy of emotion (e.g. whenever he sees himself described as a 'bland Fifties pop star'), he shouts out 'Oh, Boone!'. Anyone who's heard his records will know what he means.

Bluest of the Blues

To innocent white ears, 'the dozens' sounds like a card game – like a cross between poker and housey-housey. To African-Americans in the decades before television was invented, it was a primary form of entertainment, which could range from totally above-board to definitely behind-closed-doors. In 'the dozens', two people – men, usually – would trade insults, until one was so beaten down by the other's brain-scrambling flights of verbal invention that he sacrificed his pride and admitted defeat. It was the midway point, if you like, between the 'flyting' of sixteenth-century Scotland and the battle raps of the 1980s.

As a purely oral art form, the dozens lived in the moment: even the creators probably couldn't remember their best lines five minutes after they'd been thrown across the bar-room (especially if there was moonshine on the menu). Perhaps the closest we can get to reliving the golden age of the dozens is to cock an ear to 'Say Man', a 1959 recording by the American R&B maestro Bo Diddley; or its successor, 'Say Man, Back Again'. But both those tracks are decidedly tame by comparison with the peaks of sexual innuendo and foul-mouthed flippancy that could be heard when there was no white recording manager in the house.

The same issue afflicted a 1929 session by the blues piano player Rufus Perryman, masquerading for the occasion as Speckled Red. He recorded not one but two versions of a tune called 'The Dirty Dozens', each of which was saucy, to say the least, and certainly laced with the hints and spices of sexuality, but entirely free of any language that might need to be snipped by the censors.

In blues clubs, Perryman and his peers took several steps over the line. Audiences in back-country bars in the early Thirties lapped up tunes that laid their fornicating credentials right down on the table, regardless of who was watching. The challenge on the rare occasions when they were in front of a microphone was to retain the thrill of talking dirty about sex, without letting the boss man know what he was paying for.

Another blues pianist, Roosevelt Sykes, was renowned for his salty tale of a 'Dirty Motherfucker', who was always 'eating pussy'. As recorded for a 78 rpm single in 1936, the song was refined, but only slightly: the leading man was now a 'Dirty Mother for You', Sykes sliding the words together to leave his intentions clear. A similar transformation was waiting for a rousing bar-room blues stomp originally written as 'Drinkin' Wine, Motherfucker, Goddam' by guitarist Sticks McGhee. Unable to concoct a plausible substitute for the twelve-letter word, McGhee invented a nonsensical ten-letter one, 'spo-dee-o-dee' – and landed himself one of the biggest blues hits of the Forties.

When the blues was 'rediscovered' by white scholars and collectors, the survivors of the pre-war era were finally able to come clean (or, in this instance, dirty). Speckled Red laid down his original 'Dozens': 'Your sister loves to fuck and your brother sucks dick'. Lightnin' Hopkins added his 'Dozens' to a monologue addressed to a 'dirty black motherfucker'. But for the fullest exposition on the subject of 'The Dirty Dozens', we are indebted to blues piano player Jelly Roll Morton. When he was interviewed by the archivists of the Library of Congress way back in 1938, he told the government men everything he knew about the blues, their background, and the songs that were too risqué to be committed to record. As he soaked himself in whisky, his renditions grew ever more blue, in every sense of the word. His 'Dirty Dozens' included such poetic flights of fancy as this: 'I said, look up bitch, you made me mad/I'll tell you about the fuckers that your sister had . . . She fucked a hog, she fucked a dog/I know the dirty bitch would fuck a frog'. Dirty Mothers don't come any dirtier than that.

Lady Chatterley's Lawyer

We are indebted to Mr Mervyn Griffith-Jones, counsel for the prosecution, representative of Queen and country, for this illuminating piece of arithmetic. 'The word "fuck" or "fucking" occurs no less than thirty times. I have added them up, but I do not guarantee that I have added them all up. "Cunt" fourteen times; "balls" thirteen times'; "shit" and "arse" six times apiece; "cock" four times; "piss" three times, and so on.' After which Mr

Griffith-Jones made the unfortunate suggestion to the members of the jury that they should 'view those passages', without specifying exactly which ones he had in mind.

He was appearing at the Central Criminal Court at London's Old Bailey, before Mr Justice Byrne, on 20 October 1960 in the notorious case of Regina vs. Penguin Books Limited. At issue was the legal status of one of the most famous novels of the twentieth century: *Lady Chatterley's Lover*, by D.H. Lawrence. Was it, as Mr Griffith-Jones and his team sought to prove, an Obscene Publication, under the terms of the 1959 Act of that title? Or was it, as argued by the defence, a controversial work which nonetheless merited publication on the grounds of literary merit?

The resulting case became as celebrated as Lawrence's book, not least for Mr Griffith-Jones's questions to the jury: 'Would you approve of your young sons, young daughters – because girls can read as well as boys – reading this book? Is it a book that you would have lying around in your own house? Is it a book that you would even wish your wife or your servants to read?'

Lady Chatterley's Lover was not the first of Lawrence's books to have aroused such concern. Copies of *The Rainbow* (1915) were seized by Scotland Yard a few weeks after publication; more were destroyed after a hearing at Bow Street Police Court. Its sequel, *Women in Love* (1920), was described by *John Bull* magazine as 'A Book the Police Should Ban . . . Loathsome Study of Sex Depravity'. But neither furore approached the intensity of the firestorm that surrounded the publication – or, more accurately, intended publication – of *Lady Chatterley's Lover*.

Lawrence had completed an initial draft of the book in a remarkable forty-day spurt of creativity in the autumn of 1926; then immediately spent a further three months on a totally revised manuscript. Still unsatisfied, he returned to the sexual exploits of the lady with the emasculated husband, and a potent gamekeeper living conveniently in the grounds, at the end of 1927. By early January 1928, the book was finished, and Lawrence submitted it to his publishers in London and New York – both of whom declared that it was impossible to publish, on account of both its language and its vivid sexual descriptions. Instead, Lawrence allowed a publisher in Florence to print a small run of the uncensored text, most copies of which (and of the subsequent pirated editions) found their way back to Britain. The ever-reliable *John Bull* was quick to exploit the occasion, pronouncing that *Lady Chatterley's Lover* was 'Shameful – A Landmark in Evil', and adding, 'The sewers of French pornography would be dragged in vain to find a parallel in beastliness.'

Lawrence had his own distinctive views on the nature of pornography, French or otherwise. 'I find *Jane Eyre* veering towards pornography,' he wrote. 'As soon as there is sex excitement with a desire to spite the sexual feeling, to humiliate it and degrade it, the element of pornography enters . . . The greatest of all lies in the modern world is the lie of purity, and the dirty little secret.' The crime of Lady Chatterley, and her chronicler, was to expose the existence of sexual feeling, among the aristocracy as well as the lower classes, and to do so without shame.

In his original draft, however, her ladyship seems strangely innocent of the F-word and its power. When her lover, Mellors, describes himself as her 'fucker', Lawrence notes: 'The word, she knew from [her husband], was obscene, and she flushed deeply and then went pale. But since the word itself had so little association to her, it made very little impression on her.' She is soon employing the term herself, echoing Mellors's rhetorical question: 'Why shouldna I fuck thee, when we both on us want it?'

In the final draft, Connie Chatterley first hears the F-word from one of her husband's drinking buddies, Tommy Dukes:

75

'Love's another of those half-witted performances today. Fellows with swaying wrists fucking little jazz girls with small-boy buttocks, like two collar studs!' It is left to Mellors to introduce her to another taboo term, whereupon Connie exclaims: '"Cunt"! It's like "fuck", then.' 'Nay, nay,' Mellors replies. 'Fuck's only what you do. Animals fuck. But cunt's a lot more than that. It's thee, dost see?' In his fearless use of language, Mellors clearly speaks for his creator: 'I believe especially in being warm-hearted in love, in fucking with a warm heart. I believe if men could fuck with warmth, and the women take it warm-heartedly, everything would come all right. It's all this cold-hearted fucking that is death and idiocy.'

Before long, everyone in the novel is using the word, including Connie's husband and her father ('I never went back on a good bit of fucking myself'). But the king of 'fucking' remains Mellors, who in his final missive to Lady C combines earthy expression with Lawrentian poetry: 'We fucked a flame into being. Even the flowers are fucked into being between the sun and the earth.' As Lawrence noted in an accompanying essay, 'The words that shock so much at first don't shock at all after a while.'

Yet the taint of 'obscenity' remained. Lawrence wrote, 'Nobody quite knows what the word "obscene" itself means, or what it is intended to mean: but gradually all the old words that belong to the body below the navel have come to be judged obscene. Obscene today means that the policeman thinks he has a right to arrest you, nothing else.'

Although Lawrence himself was not arrested for the crime of writing obscenity – his punishment came in the toll that the scandal took upon his health, and in his death in 1930 – his book endured more than thirty years of censorship and repression. It was trimmed of its more controversial words for UK and US publication in 1932. In 1944, the American publisher Dial Press returned some of the taboo terms to the text, albeit as 'f---' and 'c---', and were immediately convicted of obscenity – a verdict overturned later that year. All three drafts of the manuscript appeared uncut in Italy in 1954. Then, in 1959, Grove Press in New York dared to give the full text of Lawrence's preferred version its first airing in an English-speaking country. Copies were impounded by the police, but after a series of trials, *Lady Chatterley's Lover* was finally freed from its legal shackles.

The next scene took place in London, where in August 1960 Penguin Books planned to issue *Lady Chatterley's Lover* as an unexpurgated paperback, priced at three shillings and sixpence (slightly more than the average price of a novel at the time). Anticipating that there might be legal opposition to the book, they effectively consented to the trial at the Old Bailey. A parade of expert witnesses was arranged by the defence, each taking the stand to declare that Lawrence's stature as a novelist made all talk of obscenity irrelevant. The pioneering sociologist Richard Hoggart tried to dispel the idea that the common people of Britain might be unfamiliar with Lawrence's language. 'Fifty yards from this court this morning,' he testified, 'I heard a man say "fuck" three times as he passed me. He was speaking to himself and he said, "Fuck it, fuck it, fuck it" as he went past. If you have worked on a building site, like I have, you will find they recur over and over again.'

It was Lawrence's own use of repetition that appears to upset Mr Griffith-Jones, who was forced to go through the manuscript like a trainspotter. 'Just glance down,' he told one witness. '"Cunt" appears again. "Fuck" appears. "Fuck" appears. "Cunt" appears. "Fuck" appears. All in the space of about twelve lines. Is this realistic conversation?' To which the best answer might have been: 'It is in our house, mate.'

Later, Griffith-Jones read aloud one of the most graphic sex scenes from the novel – presumably, by his own logic, thereby corrupting everyone in the courtroom – and then asked the jury: 'You would have to go, would you not, some way in the Charing Cross Road, in the back streets of Paris, even Port Said, to find a description of sexual intercourse which is perhaps as lurid as that one?' Having helpfully been supplied with a list of places where they might easily find pornographic books, the jury retired, and returned with a verdict of 'Not guilty'.

Penguin were now free to publish *Lady Chatterley's Lover*, which they did in November 1960. The entire print run of 200,000 copies was sold out on the first day, thanks in great part to the free publicity provided by Mr Griffith-Jones and his chums. Lawrence was legal; so was the F-word. After that, as Louis the Frenchman would say, it was time for *le déluge*.

Mothers

Mother Comes First

Mothers – like 'em or not, we simply can't do without them. Not if we want to be born, that is. Fathers? They might rule the universe – one of them might even have created it, if you believe the Bible – but ultimately they're dispensable. After all, nobody ever wrote a song called 'Father, the King of My Heart', 'Father and Child Reunion' or even 'Sylvia's Father'.

The mother's unique role in our lives, and our culture, explains why her name is attached to some of the most piercing insults in any language. In the Christian belief system, Mary the mother of Jesus holds a unique place: the spotless, virgin bearer of the Son of God, revered by all sects and strands, worshipped by the world's billion-plus Catholics, painted across the centuries as the ultimate manifestation of innocence and devotion. The holy respect shown to Mary in Catholic nations is reproduced in the equally fervent way in which they (especially their male inhabitants) openly admire their own mothers. So it's not surprising that languages such as Spanish and Italian are so rich in invective bent on defacing that eternal love: all the variants on *tu madre* or *tua madre* that revolve around the blameless mother suffering the most degrading of fates. When Mexican

81

men spit 'chinga a tu madre' at each other, they're not only inviting their rivals to copulate with their maternal parents, but insulting both the recipient of the verbal assault and the absent matriarch. In English, 'up your mother' doesn't quite hold the same sting.

There's another, pre-Christian strand of mother-related defilement which has also left its mark. The Greek myth of Oedipus – who, you will recall, succeeded in killing his father and then marrying (and having four children with) his mother – has passed into our global culture both as a psychological diagnosis (the Oedipus complex) but also a mythic tendency that holds an uncanny sway over our relationships with our parents, and male development from child to man. There's a parallel impulse, in which sons' love for their mothers is matched by that of daughters for their fathers (both assumed to be inescapable by many parents), but the latter does not require the daughter to kill her mother; only to leave her in the shade.

Sigmund Freud first identified the Oedipus complex at the very end of the nineteenth century; which was also the moment when a variant on that theme, and on the age-old insult from the Catholic lands along the Mediterranean, inspired the birth of a new word in the English language: one that was intended to be uniquely offensive, but which was tamed and even subverted during the second half of the twentieth century. Enter . . . the Motherfucker.

As recently as 1991, etymological expert Geoffrey Hughes observed that 'motherfucker' was first noticed by those who devote their lives to chronicling the changing shape of our language in 1956. But subsequent research has pushed that date further and further back: it might not have taken its place in 'literature' until well after the Second World War, but it could have been heard on the streets of major American cities, often from the mouths of young African-American males, well before the First World War. Court reports from the 1890s quote variants on the word cropping up in evidence ('and then he called me a motherfucking so-and-so, your honour'); which suggests that the term was probably active some time before that. Given that 'fuck' had been in use for centuries, and the idea of intercourse with one's mother was an obvious taboo (illegal, too, in almost all cultures), it is not difficult to imagine how a barrage of insults suggesting that one's enemy ought to go and 'fuck your mother' could provoke the reply: 'Who are you calling a motherfucker, mister?'

One fact is instantly apparent. There is no tradition, in English or any other major language, of 'motherfucker' being rivalled by a male-oriented equivalent: no urban streets resound to the cry of 'Fatherfucker!', in other words. That's not to say that intercourse with a father is looked upon any more lightly than the maternal version: it's still a taboo, still illegal, still every bit as likely to produce a genetic mutation if the coupling results in a child. But as the 'father' in any 'fatherfucker' is taken to be impervious to insult, that word would only carry a fraction of the weight delivered by a righteous cry of 'motherfucker'. The ultimate proof can be found in that infallible (well, maybe not entirely) judge of all modern debates, Google, which turns up 13,700,000 results for 'motherfucker', but only 379,000 for 'fatherfucker'.

The Forgotten Father

Even if 'fatherfucker' is largely absent from the English vocabulary as an insult, it has peeked its head shyly into the culture in recent years. Its most notable appearance was as the title of an album by the American singer-songwriter Peaches: a choice that might restrict her chances of radio airplay, you might think, but then the creator of such delicate offerings as 'Fuck the Pain Away', 'Lovertits', 'Shake Yer Dix', and 'Tent in Your Pants' had probably already decided to sacrifice such an obvious means of publicity.

Fatherfucker is also the literal translation of a prize-winning 1990s novel by Japanese author and artist Shungiku Uchida, though the book has yet to be rendered into English.

Neither of these works has rivalled the distribution and popularity of the American animated feature film, *South Park: Bigger, Longer & Uncut*. A musical based on the antics of several foul-mouthed schoolboys, one of whom has the unfortunate habit of dying, the movie included several songs that planted themselves immediately into the memory, such as 'Kyle's Mom's A Bitch' and 'Blame Canada'. Neither, however, could rival the impact of Terrance and Phillip's 'Uncle Fucka' – an expletive-rich show-tune which not only featured a flatulent duet during the song's bridge, but also welcomed a fresh insult into the world. As one of the cartoon parents says: 'Well, what do you expect? They're Canadian.'

The Superior Mother

The Mother Superior of a convent, otherwise known as the Abbess, should be a stern but dignified figure: the epitome of religious devotion and sinlessness. But, to satirists in the seventeenth-century, Mother Abbess was sometimes used as a euphemism – an obscure one, it's true – for a common prostitute. A variant was Mother Midnight, the popular term for a midwife, who would presumably watch over the streets while all decent nuns were asleep.

From there, it was a short slip down the ladder of decency for Mother Abbess, in the bawdy sense, to be shortened to 'Mother' – therefore giving this loveliest of English nouns a decidedly sexual bent, several hundred years before the first 'motherfucker' was ever recorded.

Mother's Multi-Tasking

Seize the Time was the rip-roaring autobiography of Bobby Seale – co-founder of the Black Panther Party, and one of the figureheads of the late Sixties revolutionary counter-culture that drove US President Richard Nixon to the brink of breakdown. So dangerous was Seale in the establishment's eyes that when he was placed on trial for conspiracy – that's conspiracy with a bunch of white radicals whom he had never actually met – he was bound and gagged in the courtroom, to prevent him spouting his righteously radical rhetoric within the delicate earshot of the judge.

Seale's book perfectly captured the anger, antagonism and sense of injustice that fuelled the Black Power movement. But it also proved its author to be unexpectedly interested in the finer points of African-American language.

The book opens with a vivid account of Seale's reaction to the assassination of Black Power leader Malcolm X in 1965. His instinctive reaction is violent rebellion, so he collects six loose bricks, 'and broke the motherfuckers in half'. Each time a police car glides down the street, he picks up a half-brick, and 'threw it at the motherfuckers'. In summary, then, 'They're driving down the street, and I'm throwing bricks for a motherfucker'. This naturally inspired Seale's imagination to dream of the day when 'I'll make my own self into a motherfucking Malcolm X'. And all of this on the first page.

So, to recap: the police are motherfuckers, which is bad; the bricks are motherfuckers, but they're Seale's bricks, so they're good; he's throwing like a motherfucker, which is presumably an expression of power; and he wants to become a motherfucking Malcolm X, which is that power redoubled to the ultimate degree. No wonder that at the conclusion of the book, Seale declares: 'Motherfucker is a very common expression nowadays.' And he quotes no less an expert on the subject than his fellow radical (and future born-again Republican), Eldridge Cleaver: 'I've seen and heard brothers use the word four and five times in one sentence and each time the word had a *different* meaning and expression.'

Yet Seale does more than demonstrate the 'motherfucker' in action: he offers an origin for the word that you won't find in any dictionary. 'Motherfucker', he declares, 'actually comes from the old slave system, and was a reference to the slave master who raped our mothers, which society today doesn't want to face as a fact.'

None of this means any insult to mothers, Seale insists: 'This never enters a black brother's mind.' Indeed, 'Raping our mothers was fantastically derogatory.' But, he concludes, 'Today, one can use the word to refer to a friend or someone he respects for doing things he never thought could be done by a black man . . . it's kind of a real complimentary statement to a brother or even a sister when one vicariously relates to someone who's black and pulls a fantastic feat. We will joyfully say, "Man, he's a mother-fucker."' Which is how a word that was rooted in barbarity came to be turned upside down, and remade into a weapon against the men that it originally described.

The Mother of All Inventions

Frank Zappa was rock music's closest equivalent to comedian Lenny Bruce: effortlessly fluent and inventive with words and music, and seized with the irresistible desire to provoke and poke fun at all forms of received wisdom and recognised authority. When his 1964 garage band The Soul Giants mutated into some-thing approaching commercial form (albeit only in a twisted universe), he required a more distinctive and compelling name for his fiendish crew.

The result? The Mothers, which (in a precursor of country stars calling themselves outlaws and rappers claiming the title of gangsta) not only accepted all the random insults that their (for 1965) outlandish appearance and abrasive style were likely to provoke, but trumped them. It was an era when record companies no longer understood what the children of America wanted to hear, or indeed why, and so they were prepared to take risks that would have been unimaginable even a year earlier. Hence the contract offered to Zappa's crew by Verve Records, conditional on one demand: that Zappa change their name from the Mothers (which, it was clear even to a company executive, was intended to be an abbreviation for Motherfuckers).

Five years later, with fame and a degree of wealth under his belt, Zappa would probably have told Verve to 'mother off'. But the prospect of widespread distribution for his uncompromising art was impossible to dismiss, and so he turned for inspiration in his necessity to the dictionary of proverbs – and recalled that necessity was, after all, the mother of invention. Which is why it was the Mothers of Invention who released rock's first double-record set in 1966, only resuming their original title again in 1971, by which time Zappa and the Mothers were more famous than the word 'motherfucker', and their name signified only success, not obscenity.

Can You Hear Me, Mother?

A Glossary of M/F-ing Euphemisms

No matter how much you love your mum, it's not always safe to tell the world about it – particularly if you're trying to show an X-rated movie on prime-time TV. Some of the following replacements might prove useful.

87

F**k

LITTLE SUCKER: from the tame redubbing of the *Pulp Fiction* soundtrack broadcast on television.

MONKEY-FIGHTING: 'I have had it with these monkey-fighting snakes . . .'

MONDAY TO FRIDAY: '. . . on this Monday to Friday plane.' Samuel L. Jackson, as edited for US television viewers.

MOTHER: simple, basic, but open to misinterpretation, especially at home.

MOTHERBEATING: compare 'beating the meat', not 'beating (by) your mother'.

MOTHERBUGGER: a *News of the World* journalist goes home for the weekend.

MOTHERCHUCKER: has an allergic stomach reaction to the very idea.

MOTHERCHUGGER: asks his mom to support a charity.

MOTHEREATING: not really helping matters: compare MOTHERSUCKER.

MOTHEREFFER: who are you calling a cow, son?

MOTHEREM: Rotherham's red light district.

MOTHERFEELING: the Oedipal version of foreplay.

MOTHERFERYER: obscure, until you compare the song title, 'A Real Mother For Ya'.

MOTHERFLICKER: the flicker is a bird from North America.

MOTHERFLUGER: ingenious substitute heard in the TV version of the movie *Heartbreak Ridge*.

MOTHERFLUNKER: she failed her Mom exam.

MOTHERFOULER: as used by distinguished novelist Ralph Ellison, author of *Invisible Man*; makes sex sound strangely dirty.

MOTHERFRIGGER: that's 'frig' in the copulatory rather than masturbatory sense, of course.

MOTHERFUGGER: Norman Mailer's father.

MOTHERFUNKER: as two words, the title of a beer brewed in California.

MOTHERFUYER: see MOTHERFERYER.

MOTHERGRABBER: another literary euphemism from the Sixties; immortalised in the song title 'Temporary Mother Grabber'.

MOTHERHOPPER: an offspring of MOTHERJUMPER, with no direct sexual meaning.

MOTHERHUBBER: another 'clever' piece of censorship of a Hollywood movie for US TV: *Pulp Fiction* again.

MOTHER HUBBARD: as utilised by John Lennon on his *Imagine* album; from the nursery rhyme, obviously.

MOTHERHUGGER: like a treehugger, but closer to home.

MOTHERHUMPER: as used by rock'n'roll star Jerry Lee Lewis in almost every song he's performed on stage since the 1970s.

MOTHERING: what mothers do, in every sense of the word.

MOTHERJIVER: extending the 'mess-with-people's-heads' strand of the F-word.

MOTHERJUMPER: that's 'jump' as in the charming phrase, 'I'd like to jump your bones'; several degrees more sexual than MOTHERHOPPER, in other words.

MOTHERLOVER: direct and to the point, yet at the same time less direct than the full M/F. Who doesn't love their mum?

MOTHERLUMPER: for the person too shy to say MOTHERHUMPER.

MOTHEROO: only suitable if you're dressed in baby clothes.

MOTHERPLUGGER: another overt sexual euphemism: plugging the gap, male or female.

MOTHERRAMMING: and they say romance is dead.

MOTHERRAPER: a subtlety-free zone, imposing force on an act that might otherwise have been consensual.

MOTHERRUBBER: at least she won't get pregnant.

MOTHERSUCKER: a euphemism that isn't much of a euphemism at all, but merely varies the plan of attack.

MOTORCYCLE: usually a 'bad motorcycle', as in the minor Sixties hit of that name: 'I knew by the way he spoke, he was a bad motorcycle.'

MOTORSCOOTER: as above, but cheaper and easier to control.

MR FALCON: an ingenious TV substitution for a Bruce Willis expletive in *Die Hard 2*.

Up Against the Wall, Mother!

It was the day after the Woodstock rock festival in August 1969, and talk show host Dick Cavett – a groovy but hardly hippie 32-year-old – had invited survivors of the festival onto his prime-time ABC-TV programme. Members of Crosby, Stills and Nash and Jefferson Airplane mingled with fans who had made the muddy journey back from Max Yasgur's farm to the heart of Manhattan, and performed material they had aired in front of hundreds of thousands of people that weekend.

Premiered during the show was a Jefferson Airplane song that had already, three months before its release on their *Volunteers* album, raised the hackles of their record company. 'We Can Be Together' was nothing less than a radical manifesto of revolt against the system, substantially based on a text from an underground newspaper. At the heart of its rousing chorus was a phrase familiar to the counter-culture, but never aired before in the mainstream: 'Up against the wall, motherfucker'. Perhaps because the song was new, and therefore unfamiliar to both the host and his production team, or because only those under the age of thirty could decipher the Airplane's lyrics with ease, their live performance continued without hindrance and censorship. Which makes vocalist Grace Slick the first person, as far as anyone knows, to have spoken or sung the F-word on American network TV.

But where was this wall, and why was the mysterious mother-fucker being told to get up against it? Several months earlier, exactly the same phrase had formed the battle cry of the MC5's song 'Kick Out the Jams', recorded live in concert in October 1968. Once again, there was alarm at the record label, who insisted that before they would release the song as a single, the MC5 should re-record the offending line as 'Kick out the jams, brothers and sisters'. The band were managed by John Sinclair, a political revolutionary from Ann Arbor, Michigan, whose White Panther Party proposed a simple manifesto involving 'total assault on the culture by any means necessary, including rock and roll, dope and fucking in the streets'. They in turn borrowed the 'up against the wall' slogan from their brothers in the Black Panther Party; but it didn't originate with them.

Earlier in 1968, a group of anarchist revolutionaries in New York City had taken to signing off their pamphlets and press releases with a defiant 'Up against the wall/Motherfucker'. As that was usually the only identification on their literature – bar an occasional reference to the 'International Werewolf Conspiracy' – the group became known by that slogan, or as the Motherfuckers for short. The anarchists had previously been known as Black Mask, and their leader, Ben Morea, has since explained that they never intended to be known as the Motherfuckers, but rather operated as 'The Family' (though that name never appeared on any statements they issued).

That spring, 'Up against the wall motherfucker' was seen as graffiti on the walls of American colleges, where student protests against oppression and the Vietnam War were rife. Student leader Mark Rudd even delivered the phrase in an open letter to the President of Columbia University in New York. And it was Rudd who let slip the ultimate source for this most durable piece of late Sixties radical rhetoric: a poem by the militant poet and playwright LeRoi Jones (who adopted the name Amiri Baraka in 1967).

'Black People' was not a poem in the conventional sense, but a prose monologue operating as a rallying cry for Baraka's fellow African Americans. It juxtaposed white Americans, who owned property and artefacts, with their black counterparts who had nothing: 'Money don't grow on trees no way, only whitey's got it, makes it with a machine, to control you, you can't steal nothing from a white man, he's already stole it, he owes you anything you want, even his life. All the stores will open if you will say the magic words. The magic words are: Up against the wall motherfucker this is a stick-up!' The poem climaxes with a stark yell of rebellion: 'We must make our own World, man, our own world, and we can not do this unless the white man is dead.' So that was the wall, the wall against which the firing squad traditionally places its victim; and the white race was the 'motherfucker', destined to take its place before the gun as recompense for its crimes. No sex in this definition, then, but plenty of violence.

Movies for Mother's Day

BANANA MOTHERFUCKER (Portugal, 2011): sixteen minutes of comic shenanigans, based around the premise that the deadliest weapon in the world is a banana. Don't miss the scene based on John Hurt's stomach cramps in *Alien*.

COLONEL KILL MOTHERFUCKERS (US, 2008): 'Revenge is a motherfucker' is the strapline for this comedy horror outing. Set in 'the peaceful town of Strangeville', it is a cavalcade of over-acting and non-existent effects, shot on a budget so low that you'd put your back out trying to pick it up off the floor. Best seen if you satisfy all the following criteria: (a) you're under 30; (b) you're, like, totally wasted; (c) you're one of the cast.

MERRY CHRISTMAS, MOTHERFUCKER (Italy, 2005): What is it about the M/F that brings out the horror psychos? It's Christmas, and a guy who doesn't believe in Santa Claus kills and eats Santa's Little Helper (not to be confused with Bart Simpson's dog). This ten-minute drama was issued on a compilation DVD with such equally enticing shorts as *The Lick-It Man*, *Teenage Bikini Vampire*, and *Revenge of the Killer Meat*. Tasty.

MOTHERFUCKER: A MOVIE (US, 2007): The changing face of a horrendously hip bunch of Manhattan 'underground' socialites, musos, and performance artists, as documented in a movie that is even less fun than attending one of their parties. Worth keeping in the closet in case you have a house guest who won't leave.

Embarrassments

Holy Cock-Up, Batman!

In the days before the computer and the mobile phone rendered the rest of the world too boring for kids to tolerate, fresh-faced youngsters devoted their time and their parents' small change to the healthy pursuit of collecting trading cards – from boxes of cigarettes (not quite so healthy) or sugary cereals, packs of bubble-gum, or simply shrink-wrapped sets of the cards themselves. Children would attempt to complete the set, by any means necessary, frequently stooping to petty violence and other forms of criminality to persuade little Johnny in Year 2 to hand over the last remaining card required to fill their album.

It was an innocent enough pleasure, providing you overlooked the violence, the theft, and the manufacturers' clever ruse of limiting the supply of a couple of the cards in each set, ensuring that desperate completists were forced to buy more and more boxes and packs in vain pursuit of their grail. And if you also ignore those ultra-violent sets of cards portraying Nazi war crimes and other atrocities that provoked tabloid press outrage, and prompted schools to institute full-body searches to ensure that no five-year-olds entered the playground with an illicit Mickey Mouse card concealed about their person.

Life proceeded quite smoothly in this way until 1989, when US baseball player Bill Ripken, an infielder with the Baltimore Orioles, posed for his slice of trading card immortality with his bat raised over his right shoulder. This exposed what Americans call the 'knob' of the bat, on which were clearly scrawled two words: 'FUCK FACE'.

It beggars belief that even in a semi-industrial business like the American trading card racket, nobody at the publishers noticed this unseemly addition to Ripken's uniform. But the photo was printed, and the card was issued – and suddenly Ripken was more famous for his bat than his batting. Quizzed by a scandal-hungry media for an explanation, he immediately fingered his team-mates: 'It appears I was targeted. I know I'm kind of a jerk at times. I know I'm a little off. But this is going too far.'

The publishers worked overtime to withdraw and censor the offending cards, though not before many thousands had been sold. The brouhaha sent demand for the 'FUCK FACE' card soaring, and prices with it; inevitably triggering turf wars, more criminality, and heartbreaking stories about first-grade kids being tricked out of their priceless heirlooms by unscrupulous 10-year-olds. To this day, an entertaining website (billripken.com) exists, to track all the variations of Ripken's card in circulation, and offer some amusing artefacts in a similar vein – cards devoted to such unlikely baseball stars as Dick Pole and Rusty Kuntz, for example.

Finally, almost twenty years after Ripken's believe-it-or-not explanation of his mishap, the infielder came clean: he HAD, after all, written 'FUCK FACE' on the end of his bat, but only so he would be able to recognise his practice bat if he needed it in a hurry, and it was standing in a crowd of other bats, and he didn't

realise until the picture came out . . . yeah, right. Still 'a little off',
Bill . . .

I'm Still Swearing

There are four letters in 'John', and four letters in most of the
words that escape from the mouth of Elton of that ilk when he
embarks on one of his legendary tiara-tossing tantrums. A particularly magnificent example of the species circulates among fans, in
the shape of the video feed from a 1992 concert in Argentina. A
minor malfunction on his electric piano gradually assumes such
monumental proportions that Elton is eventually forced to
perform while simultaneously subjecting one of his roadies to the
mother of all tirades.

Elton was in an altogether calmer mood in January 2011, when
he appeared on Chris Evans's Radio 2 breakfast show. Evans
(himself no stranger to moments of on-air madness) must have
felt that he was on safe territory when he asked his guest how
often he played the piano. To help the conversation along, he told
Elton that their mutual friend Jools Holland regularly leapt out
of bed in the morning in his eagerness to lay his hands on his
instrument. 'Oh, fucking hell,' Elton retorted, as if he'd just been
asked whether it was true that he regularly fried new-born kittens
for his breakfast. 'No, no, no,' cried his panic-stricken host, 'we
must apologise.' And so Elton did, in terms that implied that
although he had used a naughty word, anyone would have done
the same if they'd been asked whether they approached their piano
before they'd devoured their freshly fried kittens. After which there
was only one song that Chris Evans could play: 'Sorry Seems to
Be the Hardest Word'.

F**k

Licence to Ball

The phrase 'mad, bad and dangerous to know' was first applied to the poet Lord Byron, by Lady Caroline Lamb – who overcame this initial judgement of the swaggering young lothario to begin a tempestuous affair with him a few weeks later. But if Lady Caroline had been alive 150 years earlier, she could easily have decided that another poet merited the description even more: John Wilmot, the second Earl of Rochester. He was not only a central member of the 'Ballers', who sound like the seventeenth-century equivalent of the Bullingdon Club, prone to drunken revels, public brawls and screwing up the NHS; he also did his best to widen the vocabulary of English literature.

Certainly nobody before him – or for several centuries after – boasted such a long and virile sexual licence. Rochester (as we historians of the poetic art call him) was determined to give his work an immediacy that none of his peers could equal, employing the language of the gentleman (in private) and the common man (in his gutter) as his tool. Yet it is hard to resist the conclusion that the thrust of his poetic impulse was guided as much by his sheer pleasure in being a very naughty boy, as by his striving to erect a fresh pedestal for his art.

The future Earl was born on April Fools' Day 1647, into a land scarred by the mortal battle between the Puritans and the loyal Royalists commanded by King Charles. The monarch was separated from his head two years later, but Rochester's father continued to fight valiantly in the cause of the young man who would eventually be crowned Charles II. Such loyalty did not go unrecognised: when the first Earl died in 1659, and John Wilmot assumed the title, Charles vowed to watch over the lad and safeguard him from those of evil intent.

By his early twenties, Rochester was already demonstrating a peculiar facility for verse – and especially for verse that flouted the conventions of public discourse. As a result, his work was familiar only to those who heard it read aloud by its author, or who devoured the handwritten copies that were circulated among the aristocracy and intelligentsia of Charles II's court. None of his most daring work was published in his lifetime, and even after his death, his works were collected overseas rather than in London, where no respectable publisher could put his name to such risqué material.

In a 'Song' penned when he was about 24, Rochester laid his cards and his balls on the table. He portrayed a young girl, 'Fair Chloris', who lies in a pigsty and dreams of being ravished. When she awakes, she is so randy that she has only one option: she 'frigs'. One can still hear the guffaws of Rochester's audience more than three hundred years later.

His licentious creativity now knew no bounds. A year or so afterwards, he penned and circulated a riotous romp entitled 'The Imperfect Enjoyment', in which the narrator, driven to distraction by a woman's lusty appearance ('her very look's a cunt'), spills his sexual beans before he is able to manoeuvre himself into the docking procedure. The aftermath is melancholy indeed: 'I sigh, alas! and kiss, but cannot swive . . . And rage at last confirms me impotent.'

The poem climaxes with an oration of disgust at the offending organ:

> Worst part of me, and henceforth hated most,
> Through all the town a common fucking post,
> On whom each whore relieves her tingling cunt
> As hogs on gates do rub themselves and grunt.

'A Rumble in St James's Park' might sound like an Ealing Studios remake of a biker movie from the Sixties, but it actually describes impolite posh society from the vantage point of 1673, suggesting that very little changes from one century to the next: 'Much wine had passed, with grave discourse/Of who fucks who and who does worse.' His copy of Ye Olde Saucee Words was clearly well thumbed at this point, as the poem also manages to squeeze the words 'frig', 'fucked', 'swive', 'whores', 'buggery', 'bitch', 'prick', and 'cunt' into its 165 lines. And, to prove that sexism was just as rife in late-1600s social networking as it is today, Rochester coined some delightfully vivid images to describe the secret parts of a woman's form: 'lewd cunt . . . vast meal of nasty slime . . . devouring cunt'. Not the ideal young man to take home to your gran, perhaps.

Another untitled 'Song' of the 1670s imagined a dialogue between a whore and the Duchess of Cleveland – who was none other than one of Charles II's many 'discreet' lovers. The Duchess delivers one superb couplet, which would (with the politicians' names changed) carry just as much force today: 'I'd rather be fucked by porters and car-men/Than thus be abused by Churchill and Jermyn.'

The existence of this poem suggested that Rochester was not altogether careful about the way in which he treated his mentor, the King of England. Indeed, he was soon composing 'A Satyr on Charles II', of whom he wrote that 'he loves fucking much', 'rolls about from whore to whore/A merry monarch, scandalous and poor' and carried within his royal garb 'the sauciest prick that e'er did swive'. That might (just) have been acceptable to a broad-minded monarch, but Rochester's closing couplet left no doubt about his true opinions: 'All monarchs I hate, and the thrones they sit on/From the hector of France to the cully [a pal, usually uttered in derogatory terms] of Britain.'

Charles II had already been forced to turn an extremely blind eye to the young nobleman's adventures. At the age of eighteen, Rochester had taken a firm fancy to a young heiress four years his junior, but whose father (with admirable common sense) considered him to be an unsuitable match for her. So he commanded a coach-and-four and stole 14-year-old Elizabeth away from her father's house. He was tracked down and arrested; the girl was restored to her family, and Rochester sent to the Tower of London in deep disgrace and high dudgeon. The King let him stew in a fetid cell for several weeks, before setting him loose again on London's high society. So taken was young Elizabeth by his romantic gesture, incidentally, that she agreed to be his wife little more than a year later. She bore him four children, and generously provided a home for the illegitimate offspring of Rochester's liaison with a mistress.

Around 1675, several years after these escapades, King Charles II summoned Rochester to bring him a manuscript of a poem about his likely heir, the Duke of York (who took the throne as James II). 'Signior Dildo' was a singular celebration of the Duke's second marriage, which illustrated the extent to which society women, including the bride-to-be, enjoyed the company of an Italian gentleman with an unusual name, preferring his attentions to those of their husbands. Charles was prepared to be royally entertained by this verse, which was already popular among his courtiers. But instead, in a slip that Freud might have recognised, Rochester handed over a copy of his scurrilous 'Satyr' against the King.

Once he realised his mistake, the Earl assumed that his goose was cooked and his entrails would soon follow, in advance of a jolly good public quartering. So he fled the country. But within a few months he was back, having apparently been forgiven. The King even tolerated his company after Rochester had destroyed the royal sundial, although only after the nobleman had been forced to skulk in disguise for a year or two – time he devoted not to composing poetry but to masquerading as a quack doctor named Alexander Bendo. Charles's temper was presumably assuaged by the flow of risqué verse that continued from Rochester's quill, such as 'The Disabled Debauchee', in which the narrator invites a young man to join him and his female lover in bed, and then kisses them both, so he can decide 'whether the boy fucked you, or I the boy'.

There was, inevitably, another scandal on the horizon – a double-header, this time, in which Rochester and the Ballers were first said to have been discovered frolicking naked in Woodstock Park, and then took part in a mass brawl which had unfortunate consequences for a working boy who happened to stray into their path. Suddenly, as if he had reached the point of satiation, Rochester appeared to change character. His poetry retained its vividness, but lost its profanity; he talked no longer of orgies and whores but only of God and Jesus; and he declined into illness, eventually dying at the meagre age of 33. His work was still passed from hand to hand, but as tastes changed and standards of decency with them, it was first viewed as too indecent to read, and then ignored entirely. Only in more recent decades has it been considered seemly to revisit the poetry of the man who undoubtedly put the F (and several other letters) into Free Verse.

Not with a Bang . . .

Nobody embodied the pained, myopic image of the scholar more perfectly than Thomas Stearns Eliot: arguably the most influential English-language poet of the twentieth century. Thin and painfully ascetic, he suggested a man for whom the pleasures of the flesh might, on a particularly relaxed afternoon, extend to a cup of tea (no sugar) and a rich tea biscuit. The man was, after all, a banker in the days before the word became all-too-accurate rhyming slang;

then a publisher, when only gentlemen published. And still he found time to divert the course of English poetry with such peaks of modernism as 'The Love Song of J. Alfred Prufrock' and 'The Waste Land'.

At Harvard, T.S. Eliot studied philosophy for three years; then taught it for a further five. Unbeknown to his students, however, he was also scribbling verse into a notebook: some of it deathless; some of it rather less renowned, and destined only for the eyes of his closest (male) friends. With a very beady eye on the value of his success, he allowed his handwritten manuscripts to be bought by a collector in 1922, the year he published 'The Waste Land'; but first he removed several pages that might tarnish his reputation were they ever to be glimpsed by the public. Unwilling to leave them among his papers, where they might be uncovered if he should ever slip beneath the wheels of a black cab, but loth to destroy even the most insignificant of his works, he sent the offending items to someone who he knew would treasure them securely: his poetic mentor, Ezra Pound.

It was only after Pound's death fifty years later that these previously undocumented verses by the master of modernism were retrieved by archivists, and in due course offered to a grateful world as part of the definitive assemblage of Eliot's poetry. At last, his millions of admirers around the world could read 'The Triumph of Bullshit', a roaring satire on the polite literary audience, which hinged around the repeated refrain: 'For Christ's sake stick it up your ass'. On the very next page, Eliot had penned the ribald tale of 'Columbo and Bolo', which widened the great man's literary vocabulary to include 'prick', 'shat', 'whore', 'pisspot', 'cowshit', 'balls', and, for good measure, 'cock'. The fun didn't end there: Eliot introduced a character named Orlandino the cabin boy, whose 'chief remark' was 'fuck spiders!' – an exclamation rather than an instruction or complaint, and a genuine TSE extension of the English language. The poem climaxed when Columbo and the Queen 'terminated the affair by fucking on the sofa'. It was not exactly 'The Journey of the Magi'.

Eliot's career as a poetic pornographer sadly ended there, although researchers did uncover a series of 'Fragments' in which he had carefully employed the words 'fuck', 'fucked', and 'cunt', while also describing a tinker whose 'cock' mysteriously grew from two feet long to four. If *Cats* could evolve out of Eliot's feline poetry, there might also be room for some of Eliot's less familiar verses to make an XXX-rated journey onto stage and screen – 'Columbo and Bolo' the musical, perhaps. Where's Andrew Lloyd-Webber when you need him?

Je T'Aime . . . Moi Non Plus

Fame, we often hear from the famous, is a curse rather than a blessing. But there are compensations. For instance, a famous person can treat someone else – even someone as famous as they are – in ways that would land the rest of us in trouble. Or in jail.

Few celebrities ever tested that freedom with more devilish intent than Serge Gainsbourg – songwriter, singer, *bon viveur*, doyen of self-destruction, a Gallic blend of Leonard Cohen, Wyndham Lewis, and Charlie Sheen. His work was devoted to pushing boundaries, perverting clichés and *épater*-ing the bourgeoisie at every possible moment. So persistent was his desire to shock and outrage, in fact, that it was easy to overlook the genuinely courageous daredevilry of his performances and compositions.

Gainsbourg was also box-office catnip: guaranteed to provoke trouble and entertain a crowd (apart from those who were simply too shocked to be entertained). He was, therefore, one of the last people you would invite to participate in a live TV discussion, if you were trying to create something as bland as *The One Show*. Fortunately, French TV producers had a little of Gainsbourg's adventurous spirit in their own souls, which allowed the mercurial genius ample opportunities to exhibit his command of the F-word, in a variety of tongues and moods.

Exhibit *numéro un*: a 1984 appearance on a talk show, in the company of another polymath entertainer, Catherine Ringer. Before achieving musical fame with Les Rita Mitsouko, Ms Ringer earned a living as the star of adult movies with such titles as *Love Inferno* and *Body Love*. When she and Gainsbourg were forced to share a TV couch, Gainsbourg – wreathed in cigarette smoke, as ever, unshaven, joylessly disreputable – affected to find himself disgusted by Ringer's past exploits. Clearly intoxicated and (so Ringer declared) smelling like a slightly over-ripe cheese, Gainsbourg refused to look at his fellow guest, and announced his indifference to what she was saying by alternately picking his nose and mumbling vaguely incomprehensible insults: 'You're a whore . . . a prostitute . . . you get fucked by a camera'. Ms Ringer kept her cool: she had obviously met bigger pricks than Gainsbourg earlier in her career.

Two years later, another young woman was more flustered by his antics. When Whitney Houston joined him on the set of *Champs Elysées* in April 1986, she was just 22 years old, and for all the multi-platinum sales of her debut album, she looked as if she was auditioning for the role of 'Most Innocent Cheerleader' in a slasher movie. Gainsbourg was in evening dress, albeit with the air of a man who had recently been pulled from the gutter outside a particularly squalid Left Bank bar. Their subsequent conversation, moderated ineptly by the show's host, Michel Drucker, was conducted in a mixture of barrack-room French and slurred English.

F**k

Houston, entering stage left with the *naïveté* of an *ingénue* at her first junior prom, was willing to be charmed when Gainsbourg kissed her hand, and then mumbled that she was '*superbe*' (in French) and 'a genius' (in English). Then he mumbled something that didn't sound like either language. 'He says you are great,' Drucker said quickly. 'No,' Gainsbourg interrupted. 'I said, "I want to fuck her".'

Houston's reaction could be used in an acting class: this, boys and girls, is how you act surprised. She knew she had to keep smiling – this was showbiz, after all – but she couldn't hold back a frantic gasp of shock. Then, as Gainsbourg's face crumpled into self-satisfied laughter, Houston's mouth slowly formed a perfect 'O'. Way too late, Drucker intervened: 'No, he says you are great.' But Houston wasn't listening. 'Whaaaat?' she cried, before she started to laugh in disbelief. 'WHAT did you say?' So Gainsbourg repeated himself – in French, this time, to the startled delight of the audience – and then reached over to stroke her hair.

This is the point at which anyone less famous than Gainsbourg would have been carted away in *un Maria noir*. With no sign of *les flics* on the horizons, Houston was left to defend herself, flinching away from his caress. 'Sometimes he's a bit drunk, you know,' Drucker interposed, prompting Gainsbourg to violent disagreement, while Houston nervously anticipated his next advance. 'Are you sure?' she said contemptuously. 'Are you sure you're not drunk?' 'No, that's just normal,' Drucker assured her. Then the lecher resumed his assault, stretching out to stroke her chin. Houston pushed him away; then, after Gainsbourg mumbled the apologies that are the perennial defence mechanism of the habitual groper, she allowed him to kiss her hand. Gainsbourg closed the deal by fumbling with a cigarette and nearly taking her eye out, before the scene faded to black, and Houston marched off to sack the publicist who had booked her on the show in the first place.

Embarrassments

I think we can safely assume that Gainsbourg's campaign to *'baiser'* young Whitney was destined to end in failure. But maybe something about this encounter with the ultimate bad boy of French entertainment proved to be enticing, as her schoolgirl sweetness was soon banished from her public image. Within three years, she had hooked up with drug abuser Bobby Brown, and stepped onto the grim downward elevator that led to her sordid death in a Hollywood hotel room, drowning in the bath while five different drugs competed for control of her bloodstream. She might have been safer spending the night with Serge Gainsbourg after all.

Natural Gas in Space

It takes courage to be an astronaut: to sit atop a mountain of rocket fuel, and be blasted into the unknown at the whim of scientists, knowing that if something goes wrong, no parachute is going to bring you safely back to earth. So it is safe to assume that, when the ignition sequence starts, the rocket begins to roar, and the unfeasible fragile missile slowly edges off the launch pad, every astronaut with human blood in their veins is likely to be muttering a profanity or two.

The first American in space was Alan Shepard, the pilot of the Freedom 7 mission in 1961. He was a cool customer, with humour to match: asked what went through his mind as he waited for the launch, he quipped: 'The fact that every part of this ship was built by the lowest bidder.' In his autobiography, however, he recalled that he placed the biggest responsibility on himself. 'Don't fuck up, Shepard,' he whispered to himself in the loneliness of the capsule.

In public, NASA's astronauts were legendarily more circumspect. So calm and self-effacing was the leader of the first moon mission, Neil Armstrong, and so determined was he to erase any hint of heroism from his person, that in any other circumstance he would have been dismissed as terminally boring. Other astronauts who were more prone to let rip with the F-word on the ground received psychological coaching to ensure that they would be more restrained when the world was listening to their communications from space.

It is pleasing to report that, among the valiant but often personality-free men who undertook mankind's most hazardous missions, there was one hardy soul who let his humanity speak from a quarter of a million miles away. Commander John Young is a space veteran, who flew with both the Gemini and Apollo missions, and then headed up two flights by the Space Shuttle. In April 1972, he led the Apollo 16 crew, and drove the Lunar Roaming Vehicle on the surface of the moon. Yet his chief concern while he and his co-pilot, Charles Duke, rested in the Lunar Module was the state of his stomach.

To ensure that all aspects of the astronauts' digestive systems were functioning normally in the unnatural confines of the capsule, the Apollo 16 team were encouraged to feast on oranges and orange derivatives. 'I'm gonna turn into a citrus product, is what I'm gonna do!' Commander Young complained to Mission Control. The crew completed their status report, audible to everyone who was following the live TV transmissions, and then settled into what they believed was private conversation. John Young returned to the subject closest to his vitals: 'I got the farts again. I got 'em again, Charlie. I don't know what the hell gives them to me. I think it's acid stomach, I really do. I haven't eaten this much citrus fruit in twenty years! And I tell you one thing, in another twelve fucking days, I ain't never eating any more!' He was distracted for a minute, before another convulsion in his nether regions seized his attention. 'I like an occasional orange. I really do,' he said. 'But I'll be durned if I'm going to be buried in oranges.'

It was only when Young let slip another expletive – a muttered 'Oh, shit', though this time not provoked by oranges or their consequences – that Mission Control entered the conversation. 'Yes sir!' Young replied, as if snapping to attention. 'OK, John,' said the voice of Houston calmly, 'we have a hot mike.' At which point Young gathered that his musings upon the flatulent effects of the orange diet, plus the first F-word broadcast to Earth from a man on the moon, had been heard around the world. One small slip for a man, one giant linguistic leap for mankind.

F is for F-Bomb (Live on TV)

A is for ANDRETTI: Marco Andretti, American racing driver, celebrated a spectacular shunt with Sebastian Bourdais in 2011 with an equally spectacular collection of expletives, broadcast live from his cockpit.

B is for BIDEN: That's Joe Biden, the Vice-President of the United States, no less, who was overheard telling President Obama, 'This is a big fucking deal' as they signed the health care bill into law.

C is for CHRISTIAN: It's Christian Bale, of course, who was taped letting rip on a movie set with a torrent of four-letter words. Which, unfortunately, *BBC Breakfast*'s team forgot to bleep out before they broadcast an extract, much to the embarrassment of the squeaky-clean hosts.

D is for DELAY: George Michael was chatting live to Chris Evans: 'I'd be afraid of coming last on that fucking' – at which point Evans interrupted with an anguished cry of 'No, no, no!' 'You have got delay, haven't you?' Michael said. But they hadn't.

E is for EXCITEMENT: As felt by Manchester City defender Micah Richards, in his first live TV interview with the BBC's Garth Crooks: 'Fuck it, I just can't believe it!' Crooks replied like a kindly schoolmaster: 'You're a young lad, I can understand your excitement, but this is going out to a national audience, so be careful what you say.'

F is for FRAUD: On the subway, specifically: the subject on which Arthur Chi'en of CBS News was reporting when he was interrupted by a bystander. 'What the fuck is your problem, man?' he shouted, losing his job in the process.

G is for GELDOF: Exhausted by months of preparing for the Live Aid shows, Bob Geldof didn't actually tell viewers to 'just give us the fucking money'. But he did interrupt one of the live broadcast presenters to say: 'No, fuck the address, let's get the numbers.'

H is for HOLLY: And it's over to Holly Pietrzak, our anchorwoman at WDBJ: 'More teens are having fuck – having luck, rather, finding summer jobs . . .'

I is for I BEG YOUR PARDON: That was the apology from Radio 1 DJ Vernon Kay, when he accidentally referred to a 'forty-fuck artic truck'. That's 'foot', Vernon, as in 'foot in mouth'.

J is for JERSEY: The local television station, Channel TV, featured presenter Jess Dunsdon stumbling through the word 'photographer' before letting rip with an F-word, and attracting the most severe of disapproving looks from her co-host.

K is for KEATON: Veteran actor Diane Keaton was laughing at herself on US breakfast show *Good Morning America*, viewed by many millions: 'Then I'd go to work on my fucking personality.' She was much less embarrassed than her hosts.

L is for LEO: At the 2011 Oscars, Melissa Leo made a memorable acceptance speech: 'When I watched Kate [Winslet] two years ago, it looked so fucking easy – oops!'

M is for MERTON: Paul Merton has had to endure many aggravating team-mates on the BBC's 'topical news quiz', *Have I Got News For You*. But the one who appears to have made him most annoyed was Robert Kilroy-Silk, judging by the repeated cry of 'Robert, shut the fuck up!' that came from his lips. Kilroy-Silk's response? An equally repeated bellow of 'No!'

N is for NASCAR: You can always rely on American automobile racing for excitement when the action gets hot and the engines get hotter. 'You have to be fucking kidding me!' roared team chief Chad Knaus when his driver's engine blew up, and viewers heard it all.

O is for OBAMA: Not that it was the President's fault – blame Joan Rivers who, quizzed live by a CNSnews.com reporter about what she would like to tell Obama, said: 'Take care of the fucking country.'

P is for PUPPET: Basil Brush, the lovable – OK, rather annoying – fox puppet who began his BBC TV career in 1962, has worked with many 'friends' over the last five decades, but only one of them has (maybe) uttered the F-word live on TV. Stand up Barney Harwood, who was heard (or so viewers thought) muttering 'Oh fuck' live on *Basil's Swap Shop* when a kids' contest didn't go to plan. Nonsense, said his producers after the show: he actually said, 'On t'floor'. Those Lancashire accents can be tricky.

Q is for QUIT: Maybe Tom Hanks should have considered doing just that, when he appeared on *Good Morning America* to sell the film *Cloud Atlas*, admitted that one of the accents he used in the film was mostly suited to swearing, and then *still* managed to shock even himself by uttering the F-word about two seconds later. Cue the most exaggerated 'Oops' expression in acting history.

R is for REFN: Nicholas Winding Refn appeared on BBC's *Breakfast* show to promote his movie *Drive*. 'Violence is very easy to work with, cos it's a bit like fucking,' he explained. 'Oh no,' said his interviewer, 'you're not allowed to say that.' Well, he is Danish.

S is for SIMMONS: That's Sue Simmons of *Channel 4 News* in New York City, who reprimanded her backroom staff when they inadvertently put up a picture of an ocean liner as she was recording a link: 'What the fuck are you doing?' Except that she wasn't recording, she was live, prompting one of television's most heartfelt apologies: 'We need to acknowledge an unfortunate mistake that I made in one of the teasers we bring to you before this programme. While we were live just after ten o'clock, I said a word that many people find offensive. I'm truly sorry. It was a mistake on my part, and I sincerely apologise.'

T is for *TEEN JEOPARDY*: The title was apt when one contestant on the US game show failed to answer a question correctly, and instinctively groaned 'fuck', just like he would have done at home.

U is for UP: Or, as Maria Sharapova put it when a camera clicked as she was serving at a crucial point in a tennis match: 'Up your fucking ass!' But only after she'd won the point.

V is for the VIEW: While being interviewed live on TV, Susan Sarandon said: 'I had a red dress on, and red fuck-me pumps – oh, I guess you can't say that!' But she already had.

W is for WHEELER: That's half of what legendary football manager Harry Redknapp declared he wasn't in a live press conference: 'No, I'm not a wheeler and dealer. Fuck off.'

X is for X-RATED: And the most X-rated sport of all is . . . no, not football or wrestling, but the genteel middle-class pursuit of lawn tennis. Take your pick from John McEnroe telling an umpire at the Australian Open to 'fuck off', Venus Williams shooting her mouth off at Wimbledon, her sister Serena verbally assaulting a line judge in New York, or our very own Wimbledon champion Andy Murray, whose superlative skills with a racket are only matched by the vehemence with which he shouts, screams, or sometimes just mouths the F-word (and I don't mean 'foot-fault').

Y is for YOU SERIOUS: It's *Sunrise* – that's live breakfast TV in Australia. There's a phone-in contest and the hosts take a call from a woman called Jay. 'Would you like ten thousand dollars on this Thursday morning?' she is asked. 'Are you fucking *serious*?' she replies. And a line-up of highly embarrassed presenters hide their mouths behind hands, scripts and anything else they can find. 'If anybody was wondering if we're live or not,' one of them finally says with a shrug: 'we're live . . .'

F**k

Z is for Z-LIST: That's where football pundit Ron Atkinson ended up, when he told the audience watching ITV's live coverage that Chelsea player Marcel Desailly was 'what's known in some schools as a fucking lazy thick nigger'. His excuse was that he thought the microphone was turned off, but that didn't rescue his television career.

Showcases

A Class Apart

It is a truth universally acknowledged that nobody swears like a toff. Long before James Joyce and D.H. Lawrence shocked society by publishing books that committed the four forbidden letters into print, princes and earls, baronesses and ladies could casually pepper their everyday conversations with language certain to redden the cheeks of the most self-assured docker. There was mild public outrage when *The King's Speech* depicted George VI – father of our own dear Queen, let's not forget – uttering the word 'fuck' on no fewer than forty-four occasions. (Strangely enough, his stutter seemed to vanish whenever a 'fuck' left his lips. He must have been tempted to open his fateful broadcast to the British people with a hearty 'Fuck orf'.) But these were hardly the first forty-four 'fucks' to have been heard within Palace walls – or, indeed, the last.

Although Her Majesty has never been heard to utter the nation's favourite word in public (except when kidnapped by satirists or cartoonists), her devoted consort is no stranger to a good 'fuck'. His most heartfelt expletive was unleashed over the Palace speaker-phone in September 1997, directed at hapless Downing Street spin-doctors who were attempting to commandeer the arrangements for Princess Diana's funeral, and dictate what part her young sons should play in the proceedings. 'Fuck off,' the Duke of Edinburgh shouted across London with such venom that the phone was scarcely required. 'We are talking about two boys who have lost their mother!'

In less stressful times, many are the Royal engagements that have been enlivened by a *sotto voce* 'Oh fuck' from Philip when required to open yet another council office or endure one more display of ethnic dancing. His most famous outburst occurred in 1983, during a Royal visit to the United States. The limousine he was sharing with the Queen was delayed, again, by competitively anxious FBI agents guarding President Reagan and his wife. Overcome by boredom, frustration, and despair, the Duke finally cracked. 'Move this fucking car!' he screamed at the unfortunate driver in front of him, rolling up a magazine which he'd brought with him and striking the man several times over the back of his head. The driver was under orders to obey the FBI, and moved not a muscle. Neither did Her Majesty, for whom an incandescent husband was a familiar element of her right royal progress.

Rock star Ozzy Osbourne was stunned out of his usual stupor at the Queen's 2002 Jubilee Concert at Buckingham Palace, when his wife Sharon accosted Camilla with the carefully considered: 'I think you're fucking great.' While Ozzy imagined that he and his missus would be whisked straight to the Tower, Camilla took the unorthodox greeting in her stride. 'Oh, it's quite all right,' she told Sharon. 'We curse quite a lot around here.' This was confirmed by those who remember Camilla in her hunting'n'shooting prime, cantering around the fields of Berkshire astride a fearsome steed, bellowing 'Bloody hell, get out of the fucking way!' at any mortal unfortunate enough to cross her horse's path. Paparazzi beware.

This Be the Librarian

The posthumous publication of the lifetime's collected correspondence of the poet Philip Larkin uncovered a passion for pornography, and for sexual innuendo of the most inventive and/ or basic kinds, that was not immediately obvious to those who were only familiar with his tiny canon of work. Nor was it known to those respectable executives of Hull University who appointed the poet as their Head Librarian. So Larkin might have appreciated the irony that the two poems for which he seems destined to be remembered by future generations both have connotations with sex, or the language associated with it.

The first is 'Annus Mirabilis', the opening lines of which – 'Sexual intercourse began/In nineteen sixty-three' – can be quoted by thousands who have never knowingly read a complete Larkin poem. The second, from the same collection, *High Windows* (1974), is 'This Be the Verse'. Again, the title is less familiar than the opening salvo: 'They fuck you up, your mum and dad.' More than a decade after its initial appearance in print, in the journal *New Humanist*, Larkin told a friend that this was destined to be his equivalent of W.B. Yeats's 'Lake Isle of Innisfree', the piece most quoted by those who cared little for his work. 'I fully expect to hear it recited by a thousand Girl Guides before I die.' Less expected, perhaps, was its celebrated reading by an appeal court judge at the conclusion of a 2009 divorce case.

Larkin had originally posted a draft of the poem to his lover Ann Thwaite, suggesting that she might like to include it in one of the *Allsorts* selections of children's verse that she edited every year. As he told an interviewer in 1981, the poem was more complex than its first line suggested: '"They fuck you up" is funny, because it's ambiguous. Parents bring about your conception, and also bugger you up once you are born. Professional parents, in particular, don't like that poem.' He might have added that 'This Be the Verse' excused each generation of parents for their carnal and cardinal sins, because 'they were fucked up in their turn'. His concluding line – 'And don't have any kids yourself' – may have been intended as consolation or self-defence; Larkin died at the age of 63, without having fathered a child.

This was not the poet's first fling with the F-word, however. The title poem of *High Windows*, written in 1965, revised two years later and first published in a 1968 issue of the *Critical Quarterly*, was written in the voice of a middle-aged man who could 'see a couple of kids' from his remote window on the world – 'And guess he's fucking her and she's/Taking pills or wearing a diaphragm'. Here, Larkin isn't intending to startle his readership ('I don't think I've ever shocked for the sake of shocking,' he mused in 1981), but is using language with utter precision. 'Fucking' is there to express the freedom available to the modern generation which wasn't to his; elsewhere in the poem, he uses the word 'bloody' as an example of what passed for liberation when he was a young man. And both 'fucking' and 'bloody' represent only limited freedom in the context of this poem, when compared with the boundless scope of 'air'. No writer has ever used the F-word so poetically.

Fuck You, Please

A title can make a magazine, or break it before anyone has picked up its first issue. Modern publishers wouldn't dream of tossing a new journal onto the streets and into the shops without running a selection of names past marketing consultants and focus groups. The most effective titles are those which are either wonderfully vague (*Vogue, Esquire, Q*) or perfectly specific (*Railway Modeller, Homes & Gardens*). Some mags have died when their title became an anachronistic embarrassment – like *The Listener* (when most people were watching) and *Melody Maker* (when 99 per cent of the bands they were covering were deliberately trying to avoid anything as obvious as a melody). It's a rare beast that, like the *Radio Times*, can retain a name invented for a long bygone age and become such a familiar part of the language that its literal meaning has long since been irrelevant.

'A familiar part of the language' – yes, that description applies perfectly to the moniker of a journal that was launched in the spring of 1962, by an idealistic young American poet and bookstore owner in New York City. The previous year, the 22-year-old Ed Sanders had been jailed briefly for his part in a protest against the presence of nuclear missiles on American submarines. This experience sparked his poetry into life, and inspired Sanders to provide an unorthodox vehicle for maverick writers like himself, many of whom congregated at his Peace Eye Bookstore in Greenwich Village.

And so was born, on multi-coloured mimeographed paper, what was subtitled as *A Magazine of the Arts* – with the uncompromising title of *Fuck You*. That name was dubbed 'cheerily obscene' by *Life* magazine in 1967; and more than fifty years after its first appearance, it still cannot be printed in the otherwise forensically accurate pages of the *New York Times* (*Time* magazine bottled out by calling it *Love You* instead). 'My vision was to reach out to the "best minds" of my generation,' Sanders explained many years later, 'with a message of Gandhian pacifism, great sharing, social change, the expansion of personal freedom (including the legalization of marijuana) and the then stirring messages of sexual liberation.' Sanders omitted one crucial theme from his list: the playful desire to stretch poetry – and the language that could be legally carried in the pages of a magazine – way beyond its conventional limits.

F**k

The pages of *Fuck You*, which were originally filled with the writings of Sanders and a few friends, eventually grew to encompass such notable writers as Norman Mailer, Antonin Artaud, and Allen Ginsberg. It spawned a spin-off publishing house, the Fuck You Press, which 'liberated' previously unknown works by D.H. Lawrence and Ezra Pound, printed W.H. Auden's pornographic poem 'The Platonic Blow', added Lawrence Ferlinghetti's 'To Fuck is to Love Again' to the poetic canon, and provided a home for Sanders's own collection, *Fuck God in the Ass*. Sanders also issued a series of single-sheet offerings, under the generic title: 'The Fuck You Quote of the Week'.

But it was *Fuck You: A Magazine of the Arts* that made the most adventurous and creative use of the F-word and its associated activities. The first issue introduced a regular feature by Nelson Barr, 'A Bouquet of Fuckyous', a speed-written rant against anyone who had attracted his attention – often including his editor and fellow contributors. 'Send me yr goddamn manuscripts,' Sanders wrote, 'I'll print anything,' and traditional forms of censorship were sidestepped entirely. The magazine rapidly progressed from work that dropped the F-bomb as casually as the romantic poets wrote about daffodils, to altogether more abrasive and confrontational material.

The semi-anonymous Margaret X contributed 'Ronnie', in which she proclaimed her desire to save her virginity for her brother. Someone named Penny came up with a visual poem which was 'an exact replica of a vaginal smear' (her own, of course: she didn't give her surname, because 'she doesn't want her parents to know she's been fucking like a mink'). Sanders himself composed the tongue-in-cheek (as against tongue-in-sheep) 'Sheep-Fuck Poem', thereby extending the parameters of American verse into fresh fields. 'People keep informing us we've hit the absolute absolute depth of filth and corruption,' Sanders crowed. 'Balls!'

He demonstrated the point by printing a poem that momentarily caused him to doubt his own commitment to total liberation of word and thought, or at least to fear the possible consequences. 'Stark paranoia gripped the editor as he typed this stencil. Fuck it,' Sanders added to the bottom of a piece by one of his regular contributors. Al Fowler was already familiar to the hard-core readership of *Fuck You* for his unsparing chronicling of his own heroin addiction, and for Sanders's description of his sexual tastes in his list of contributors: 'Refuses to gobble or ball anything over twelve years of age.' But Fowler's 'Caroline' made his previous work seem like a Sunday School sermon. 'I saw the hot eyes of my young daughter rolling in passion,' it began, before detailing a paedophile encounter between father and child – imaginary, as Fowler had no daughter – in language that could not be repeated today unless one had a rampant desire to meet members of the Metropolitan Police's sexual offences squad.

As nobody was buying a magazine called *Fuck You* unless they already had a taste for the avant-garde, there were no complaints, no prosecutions. Thus emboldened, Sanders felt free to publish transcriptions of two taped encounters between Allen Ginsberg and his lover (and fellow poet) Peter Orlovsky: the first describing precisely what was said and groaned when Peter gave Allen a hand-job, the second leaving Allen to do the work by himself. Michael McClure, in an issue which Sanders dedicated provocatively to 'the flaming boy cock and the twelve-year-old snatch', contributed a 'Fuck Essay' which instructed the readers to 'say FUCK, say CUNT, say SHIT' (they probably already were) and described how he had used the word 'fuck' as 'a mantra to break a barrier that kept me from straight speech'.

Having already shattered all respectable standards of decency, Sanders could do nothing more than to widen the scope of his authorship, and his readership, by inviting more famous names to join the fun. (Literary scholars should note that Norman Mailer provided a poem entitled 'The Executioner's Song' a full fourteen years before he used the same title for his Pulitzer Prize-winning 'novel' about the murderer Gary Gilmore.) By the summer of 1965, when Sanders was boasting that his was 'the magazine of butt-fucking, revulsed freaks, dope dealers and group grope', and inviting his audience to sign up for a 'FUCK-IN . . . at a romantic screwable public location', to protest against the Vietnam War, his *Fuck You* antics were starting to seem no more outrageous than any of the other outlaws and misfits who were gathering under the loose heading of 'the underground'.

Yet a man who rented a post office box in the name of *Fuck You* could not be allowed to continue his unrestrained adventures indefinitely. At the dawn of 1966, his Peace Eye store was busted by the police, and numerous items confiscated. Among them was the 100 per cent non-obscene film footage Sanders had taken of his brother's wedding, and his stock of *Fuck You* back issues. Most men in his situation would have negotiated a plea bargain and accepted a fine, but Sanders enlisted the aid of the American Civil Liberties Union and fought his charges in a succession of courts, until he was eventually acquitted on all counts in 1968. But the legal hassles – plus his burgeoning career as a rock star (see elsewhere in this book) – forced him to close *Fuck You* forever.

We leave the Fuck You Press, and its 'three years of quality printing and aggressive innocence in the pornography industry', with a brief glimpse of one of Sanders's most prized publications. In 1965, Fuck You issued a pamphlet enticingly titled *Bugger! An Anthology of Buttockry*. It was, Sanders explained, a collection of 'anal erotic, pound cake cornhole, arse-freak and dreck poems'. And the normally mundane details of its publication history summed up the ethos of the Fuck You press with admirable energy:

it was, he exclaimed, 'printed, published, freaked, groped, slurped, sucked, fucked, edited, finger-stalled, supposited and ejaculated by Ed Sanders at a secret BUGGER scene'. (Fuck you – ed.)

A Message from our Sponsors

From the golden age of the F-word: here are two posters that could have graced your wall at the height of the hippie counter-culture.

(1) FUCK FOR PEACE: A simple slogan, accompanied by even simpler cartoons of mixed-race couples across the world's hottest war zones (distributed with the underground newspaper *Yeah* in 1965).

(2) FUCK HOUSEWORK: Mock-embroidered, like a granny's sampler from the nineteenth-century, with a picture of a witchy woman holding a broken broom, and the words 'Women's Liberation' forming the hem of her skirt (issued in 1971, 'for liberated women and men').

F**k the Abbreviation

FTA was an abbreviation familiar to the 'grunts', the infantrymen who were serving with the US armed forces in the Vietnam War. It stood for an attitude that, at one time or another, all but the most blinkered members of the service had shared: Fuck the Army. As such, it was the perfect name for a radical anti-war theatre group which toured America and overseas in 1971–2, playing venues as close as they could to Army bases so that service personnel could attend. As it grew, FTA began to involve many well-known names from the American entertainment industry, including Jane Fonda, Donald Sutherland, Country Joe McDonald and Nina Simone. They swore that 'FTA' actually stood for 'Free the Army', but audiences preferred to believe otherwise.

The Vietnam War was not the only conflict in the early 1970s to spawn an F-related abbreviation. Outsiders who toured the troubled streets of Belfast and Derry in Northern Ireland saw graffiti painted on walls in Protestant and Catholic districts – FTP in the former, FTQ in the latter. Locals had no problems deciphering what they meant: they could take their choice between Fuck the Pope and Fuck the Queen.

All You Need Is 'Love'

Ah, the Beatles – John, Paul, George and Ringo, the Fab Four, the Moptops, the lovable lads from Liverpool who were irrepressibly cheeky and yet unfailingly adorable. Until they started taking drugs and going all oriental, that is. And (yes, John, we mean you) sleeping with Japanese performance artists when they had a nice English wife waiting for them at home. And (John again) taking their clothes off on album covers. And (guess who?) marching through the streets of London carrying placards in support of the IRA.

Anyway, there was a brief period when it was hard for anyone who wasn't a member of parliament or a moralising columnist on a broadsheet newspaper *not* to love the Beatles. Yet beneath their shiny fringes lurked the brains of four angry young men from the North, who in keeping with the times thought nothing of utilising all the swear-words that were in common parlance, albeit not yet in the dictionary. John Lennon (him again) may have refrained from slipping them into his teenage love letters to

Cynthia Powell, who would soon become his first wife; but he had no such qualms when unloading his soul to his college friend Stuart Sutcliffe. 'I remember a time when everyone I loved hated me because I hated them,' he wrote in a 1961 letter, channelling the timeless spirit of the self-pitying adolescent. 'So what, so what, so fucking what.'

The Beatles would never have dared to use such language in public at the height of their fame: Beatlemania would have died in an instant if they had tossed around the F-word in front of impressionable teenagers. What's remarkable in retrospect is that, as early as 1964, evidence that their private speech wasn't quite as cuddly as their media image was freely available to anyone who could afford four shillings and sixpence for a paperback book.

The volume in question was *Love Me Do: The Beatles' Progress* by the American journalist Michael Braun. He accompanied the group during several of the most frenetic months of their career, during which they graduated from home-grown pop sensations to international superstars. Clearly Braun had not granted the group or their manager editorial approval of his work, and the Beatles were sufficiently relaxed in his presence to talk exactly as they would have done if he hadn't been there. And so it was that Braun was able to quote John Lennon as having uttered a word that had triggered an obscenity case at the Old Bailey just three years earlier. More strangely still, the source for his quote was actually Brian Epstein, the group's manager, who would usually have been desperate to deny any such uncouth utterances.

Here's how Braun told the anecdote: 'Epstein recalled that at the [Royal] Command performance he had asked John how he would get that kind of audience to join in. "I'll just ask them to rattle their fucking jewellery," John had said, and with obvious deletions the statement had remained, and become the Beatles' most widely quoted line.' It's a testament to the respect with which the British press regarded the group at this point that none of the London papers chose to exploit this revelation with a 'BEATLE IN FOUL-MOUTHED SHOCKER' headline.

Four years later, when the Beatles' authorised biography was published, few fans or journalists retained any illusions about the balance between the group's innocence and experience. The author, Hunter Davies, quoted George Harrison as having relished John Lennon's line, in the song 'I Am the Walrus', about a girl taking down her knickers. 'Why can't you have people fucking as well?' Harrison continued. 'It's going on everywhere in the world, all the time. So why can't you mention it? It's just a word, made up by people. It's meaningless in itself. Keep saying it – fuck, fuck, fuck, fuck, fuck, fuck, fuck. See, it doesn't mean a thing, so why can't you use it in a song? We will eventually.'

Yet when they did, smuggling the F-word into one of the best-selling singles of all time, nobody noticed. There were lots of other things to note about the record in question: it was a global chart-topper, the first release on the Beatles' own label, and it was a seven-minute pop anthem, still capable of uniting any audience in the world in a glorious singalong. But 'Hey Jude' was also something more unexpected: the home of the Beatles' first (musical) 'fuck'. To be precise, a 'fucking hell' – uttered by one of them (experts divide almost fifty/fifty between Lennon and McCartney) at precisely 2'57" into the song. The Beatles were the masters of aural chaos in 1967 and 1968, often using their fade-outs as collages of 'found sounds' ('I Am the Walrus' being the best example). On 'Hey Jude', however, they seem to have located an accidental exclamation deep in the mix, and deliberately retained it on the final single – a boyish prank or an act of artistic subversion, as you prefer.

Those impulses were neatly combined almost a year later, when George Harrison agreed to release a single by a little-known

American songwriter via the Beatles' Apple label. Stephen Friedland, who recorded under the pseudonym of Brute Force, had submitted a demo tape to Apple which included a gentle ditty about the monarch of a distant land called Fuh (rhymes with 'duh', not 'you'). As Friedland sang, 'Everybody called him the Fuh King', which was where the fun began: 'mighty, mighty Fuh King', indeed. This was as blatant as the 'Hey Jude' fuck had been discreet, and the 'King of Fuh' single received only the most limited distribution.

A decade of Beatle profanity climaxed in December 1970 with the release of *John Lennon/Plastic Ono Band*, an album of savagely personal confessional songs. It included 'Working Class Hero', in which a middle-class Liverpudlian who lived in an aristocratic mansion staked his claim to proletarian roots. In keeping with the album's theme of frankness and honesty, 'Working Class Hero' included not one but two unashamed renditions of the word 'fucking'. (Another song found Lennon clinging bravely to a single 'cock'.) After much internal debate, EMI Records, who distributed the Beatles' music, agreed that Lennon could retain the forbidden adjectives, but insisted that they should be deleted from the lyric sheet – although Lennon's diction was so clear in both instances that there was no mistaking the colour of his invective. Elsewhere in the world, notably in South Africa and Spain, the offending song vanished entirely from the record; in Australia, merely the F-words were snipped. To coincide with the album, Lennon gave an interview to the magazine *Rolling Stone* in which he set a new world record for swearing in the act of record promotion – an achievement that endured another twenty-five years until the arrival of Oasis.

Ironically, the pinnacle of the Beatles' 'fucking' career didn't involve any of the Fab Four. In the early Seventies, Tony Hendra of the comedy troupe National Lampoon took choice extracts from Lennon's expletive-rich *Rolling Stone* interview, and set them to Lennonesque music. The result was 'Magical Misery Tour', a song that begins with 'John Lennon' complaining 'I resent performing for you fuckers' and ends with a series of 'Fuck!' shrieks that descend into incoherent screaming. As the song says, genius is pain.

Not F-F-F-Fade Away

Rolling Stones Songs that Don't Eff About

(1) 'ANDREW'S BLUES': Andrew is Andrew Loog Oldham, who was ostensibly producing the early 1964 session at which this F-filled frolic was recorded. Besides the Stones, other participants included two members of the Hollies, solo star Gene Pitney, and legendary producer Phil Spector. And it was the notorious murderer-to-be who took charge of this R&B romp, which poked fun both at Oldham and at Decca Records boss Sir Edward Lewis (who is impersonated as saying, 'The Rolling Stones are a fucking good group'). Not surprisingly, Oldham didn't ask Decca to release it.

(2) 'SCHOOLBOY BLUES': The Decca hierarchy wasn't quite so lucky six years later when the Rolling Stones' contract reached its conclusion. The label informed Mick Jagger that the band still owed them one more single, so Jagger responded with this solo acoustic blues tune, more popularly known among fans as 'Cocksucker Blues'. It was the plaintive tale of a young man adrift in dirty London town, with two questions on his mind: 'Where can I get my cock sucked? Where can I get my ass fucked?' Sir Edward and his boys opted to file the track away in their archives – which is where it remained, at least until the early 1980s, when

the company's German arm included it as a bonus track in a Stones retrospective. And had their corporate 'ass' well and truly fu— sorry, smacked by the head office in London. 'Cocksucker Blues' later gave its name to Robert Frank's vivid documentary film of the Stones on tour, and also provided a fairly accurate description of the movie's contents.

(3) 'STAR STAR': By 1973, when this song was released on the *Goats Head Soup* album, the Rolling Stones were struggling to concoct the same notoriety that had been theirs by right a few years earlier. This rather jaded effort, originally titled 'Star Fucker', aimed to capitalise on their association with Hollywood's rich and famous, name-checking Steve McQueen, Ali McGraw and John Wayne in its portrayal of a rock groupie whose pet cat, if I read the lyrics correctly, was very well turned out.

The Ultimate Film Festival

The mother of all concepts, for any art-house brave enough . . .

A BEAUTIFUL FUCKING EXPERIENCE (USA, 2013): No sex, I'm afraid – just a documentary about a run of eight shows along the Mississippi Delta by the American art-rock band Flaming Lips.

BACK TO FUCKING CAMBRIDGE (Austria, 1987): This art movie was too arty for the art-houses, though its sixty minutes feature appearances from no fewer than thirty-four avant-garde artists and gallery owners. They play various members of the Viennese cultural élite circa 1900 and enact the relationships between . . . no, it's no good, I'm losing the will to live. Cambridge council should have sued them.

CORPSE FUCKING ART (West Germany, 1987): Jörg Buttgereit's catalogue of films about death, sex and (obviously) necrophilia was both celebrated and satirised in this documentary about the making of his grossest work. The movie inspired the formation of an Italian death metal band, Corpsefucking Art, whose oeuvre includes 'No Woman No Grind', in which a Bob Marley anthem is first dive-bombed and then has its brains sucked out.

DEAD FUCKING LAST (Switzerland, 2012): Films don't get any sexier than this drama about two competing firms of cycle couriers, in what is effectively a remake of *Carry On Cabby* for the post-fossil-fuel age.

FUCKING AMAL (Sweden, 2000): In which top Swedish film-maker Lukas Moodysson examines the agonised landscape of teenage sexuality and love, focusing on the embarrassment of real life rather than the fantasies of porno movies. It was released in English-speaking territories under the more multiplex-appropriate title of *Show Me Love*.

FUCKING DIFFERENT (Germany, 2005): The first in a series of portmanteau projects combining short dramas by gay film-makers. Subsequent projects were centred in particular cities: *Fucking Different New York*, *Fucking Different Tel Aviv*, and *Fucking Different Sao Paulo*. Sadly, production on *Fucking Different Bognor Regis* seems to have been terminally delayed.

FUCKING FERNAND (France, 1987): A war comedy about a blind man who wants to lose his virginity. There's nothing like the French sense of humour.

FUCKING KASSOVITZ (France, 2011): Not your usual making-of DVD extra: this documentary about the tortuous creation of the lame sci-fi flick *Babylon A.D.* features an opening scene in which the movie director introduces himself to his bewildered cast: 'I'm not Orson Welles. I'm not Steven Spielberg. I'm fucking Mathieu Kassovitz.'

FUCKING SHEFFIELD (UK, 2006): Kim Flitcroft's reality drama is a tale of junkies, lap dancers, and lots of Mods on scooters. A young woman sticks needles into every available part of her body. And someone has their teeth pulled out. Strangely, it's not mentioned on the website of the Sheffield Tourist Board.

YOUNG PEOPLE FUCKING (Canada, 2007): It sounds like an open invitation for a visit from your local police force, but it's nothing more risqué than a comedy drama chronicling the sex lives of five young couples, who are attempting in different ways to grapple with the etiquette of the erotic encounter. Also known more discreetly as *Y.P.F.*

An Actor's Tale

It's a dramatic moment at the local theatre, at some point in the last hundred years. The hero flings open the door, and finds the heroine slumped on the sofa, the marks of the strangler's hands still fresh around her delicate neck. He falls to his knees, flings his arms wide in agony, and cries out to the audience: 'What'll I do?' The response from the back of the stalls, in this much-quoted but probably apocryphal anecdote of life on the provincial theatre circuit, is short but straight to the point: 'Fuck 'er, while she's still 'ot.'

Three F-Word Steps to Heaven

There's a chart on Wikipedia – look it up for yourselves – which lists the 'Films that most frequently use the word "fuck"'. At the top is the documentary *Fuck,* which is probably cheating. In second place, with 625 usages in just ninety-six minutes, is the 2008 horror movie *Gutterballs* – the title of which is proof that sometimes the makers of a film simply can't stop themselves from reviewing their own product.

But simple statistics aren't enough. Any fool can fill an hour and a half of motion picture with the F-word: what takes skill (as anyone who's ever seen the BBC's *The Thick of It* can confirm) is to create a memorable scene out of something as everyday as swearing. With that in mind, may we bring you . . . the Three Greatest F-Word Scenes in History.

In third place, please welcome one of the most ambiguous matinee idols of all time, the romantic comedy star turned campaigner against the evils of the press: Hugh Grant. *Four Weddings and a Funeral* (1994) was the film that brought him to international fame. It opens with Grant where he is destined to end up, in bed; but this time he's alone and late for a wedding. In a scene that is repeated through the movie like a *leitmotif,* Grant is stunned into wakefulness by his alarm clock, and utters a procession of F-words as he and Charlotte Coleman stumble towards the church. He breaks up the pattern of 'fucks' with an occasional 'fuckity-fuck' and even a 'fuckadoodledoo' for light relief. But, amusing though the scene is, it's hard in retrospect to escape the feeling that screenwriter Richard Curtis is merely indulging in gratuitous use of the forbidden four letters to appear daring – a trick he has repeated, with progressively reduced impact, several times since. TV footnote: American television edits of this movie frequently replace 'fuck' with 'bugger' throughout. Somehow 'buggity-bugger' sounds ruder than 'fuck-ity-fuck'.

In second place, with a special award for concentrated profanity, it's time to accompany Steve Martin, harassed beyond human endurance, to the airport car rental desk. There, in the solitary R-rated scene of *Planes, Trains and Automobiles*, he encounters clerk Edie McClurg, trussed up like a Thanksgiving turkey, and keeping her customers waiting by chatting on the phone with her folks. When she finally greets Martin in a voice that sounds like the world's most annoying cat, he explodes into an epic fusillade of eighteen F-words in exactly a minute, only to be trumped by Ms McClurg. Once again, American TV viewers missed all of Martin's expletives: in the censored version, McClurg simply tells him that he's screwed. The fact that the scene is still funny is testament to the dramatic skills of both actors.

And our winner . . . from the censor-free HBO television network, it's a scene that not only exhibits the vast emotional range of the F-word, but also propels the action and shows off the arts of film editing and directing at their finest. I'm referring, of course, to the double-handed efforts of Dominic 'McNulty' West and Wendell 'Bunk' Pierce. In episode four of the first series of *The Wire*, two of Baltimore's finest revisit an old crime scene. Once they're inside the room where the victim died, they spend four minutes sizing up the location, uncovering lost evidence and revealing how the crime was committed, without uttering anything other than variations on the word 'fuck'. As soon as they step outside again, normal (foul) language is resumed. Contrived? Of course. But the scene is constructed with such skill, and the plot advanced with such unnoticed ease, that the cavalcade of F-words is both cunningly paced and deliciously effective. As Bunk would say: *moth*-er-*fuck*-er.

F**k

Our Special Guests This Week Are . . .

Bands who will never appear on prime-time TV:

Fuck
Fuck Off
The Fuck Ups
Fuck Buttons
The Fat Dukes of Fuck
The Fuck Off and Dies
Fuck the Blonde
Head Fuck Terrorist
Holy Fuck
Filthy Fuck
The Fuck You Man
Fuck U All
Exploding Fuck Dolls
Seething Fuck Patties
Fuck Him He's a DJ
Fuck You the Hobo Clown
Fuck the Mainstream
Suffocate for Fuck Sake
Scum Fuck Chuck
Nuclear Raped Fuck Bomb

Prohibitions

From Here to Fugging Eternity

'When I start creating characters, I have to believe in their speech as it comes out,' said the young novelist Norman Mailer when he was plugging his debut novel, *The Naked and the Dead*, in 1948. The book had already been rejected by one major publisher on the grounds of obscenity – their esteemed literary advisor telling them, 'I swear. My wife swears. In fact, my whole family swears. BUT . . .' His inference was clear. It was one thing to swear in private; another to suggest that all those secret swearers, who kept up a discreet veil of decency in public, would want to read a book filled with the same language they used at home.

Mailer had the opposite problem. His novel was set in the US Army during the Second World War, a scenario which was based on his personal experience. It captured with more realism than any previous book the atmosphere of life at war: the fear, the tedium, the divisions between officers and other ranks, and through it all the existential struggle to survive, as men and as human beings. And to tell that tale with any kind of veracity, Mailer needed his characters not only to act like soldiers, but to speak like them as well.

That's the artistic excuse for bad language in the movies, on TV, in hip-hop records: you can't show the truth without telling the truth. There are exceptions, of course. The two bizarre traits displayed by every single character in *EastEnders* are (a) they don't watch *EastEnders* or *Coronation Street*; and (b) they never swear. In real life, the F-word would comprise about 45 per cent (in a scientific estimate, which I made up a few seconds ago) of all the conversations in the Queen Vic. To compensate for this lack of foul-mouthed invective, the entire cast gets REALLY ANGRY really quickly, and SHOUTS where they would normally swear.

That's not an option for the author of a 600-page novel. Mailer needed his men to curse as casually and instinctively as the men with whom he'd served in conflict. But he knew that in the late Forties, no reputable publisher would dare to publish a book that was littered with the F-word. So he invented a replacement – a one-time-only substitute for the word 'fuck', which would sidestep an obscenity charge and yet retain the authentic flavour of the mess-room and the battlefield. What he didn't realise was that his short-term solution would enter popular culture, and the American language, and stick around for the rest of the century.

The word he concocted was 'fug'. 'I used to rationalize it to myself, right from the word go,' Mailer recalled several decades later, 'saying to myself, "They didn't really say 'fuck' in the army, they said 'fug.'" Even if I could use "fuck", I wouldn't. "Fug" works better. It's closer to the deadness of the word the way we used to say it: "Pass the fuggin' bread." So "fug" was it from the beginning.' And 'fug' it remained, from the opening chapter to the last: around 400 appearances in 600 pages, which is still pretty restrained compared to real life.

'The word never gave me any pleasure,' Mailer complained later. 'I used it because I felt that it was a fair word to use to give the quality of the Army experience . . . it was used to fill certain spaces in the thought waves that you had in the Army. In other words, it was really a way of filling gaps. It was used to give a kind of rhythm in speech. It has nothing to do with obscenity.'

Having created his stop-gap, achieved his best-seller, and invented what soon became a humorous euphemism for the real F-word among millions who had never actually read *The Naked and the Dead*, Mailer embarked on a writing career in which the confrontation of taboos, and the defiance of social conventions, were central to his art. Why else would he have directed a 1967 movie called *Wild 90* in which, he boasted, 'The language is absolutely sensational. There must be something like 500 four-letter words used in ninety minutes.' Mailer himself starred in the picture, tossing off lines like 'I could fuck a girl with my ears better than you can with your triple prick' with such evident relish that it distracted him from the serious business of making a film anyone would want to watch.

For Mailer, 'fug' and 'fugging' were two decades in the past by 1967 – a symbol of the necessary but slightly shameful compromise which he'd employed to trigger his career. But the word had long since passed out of his control. In late 1964, he'd contributed a poem to *Fuck You*, the magazine edited by his friend Ed Sanders. The following issue contained an announcement that must have taken Mailer by surprise: the arrival of a new rock band, entitled the Fugs.

Two of the creative forces behind the Fugs were Sanders himself and another, much older poet, Tuli Kupferberg. He too was a *Fuck You* contributor, who had enlivened a 1962 issue of the magazine with his poem, 'Fuck Is God'. 'I say: to masturbate is human,' it began, 'to fuck divine . . . I say fuck or die . . . I say governments oppose fucking/Because old men oppose fucking . . . I say come all ye fuckful/I say fuck is beauty/Fuck is God.'

So it was inevitable that the Fugs would not only be

unconventional as a rock band: they would also be unashamedly confrontational. An early poster demonstrated their approach: 'Fugs want to thank you,' it read harmlessly, but if it was folded carefully in keeping with their instructions, that slogan now became: 'Fuck you'. Between 1965 and 1970, the Fugs were a constant, grit-in-the-eye feature of American culture, forever tweaking the nipples of Lady Liberty and scrawling obscenities on the Flag. They were at the forefront of every major demonstration against the Vietnam War; helped to 'levitate' the Pentagon; championed the outrageous and fearless against the staid and repressed; and managed to persuade so many like-minded freaks to sign up for their cause that they propelled three albums onto the American chart.

Along the way, without any fanfare, the Fugs succeeded in becoming the first recording artists to score a hit record (albeit a very minor hit) with a bunch of songs that included the F-word. The initial run of their debut album was gently censored by their record label, who were more used to dealing with orthodox folk singers than prototype hippies with an anarchic attitude towards the conventions of songwriting (thereby pre-empting the much more celebrated Velvet Underground by at least a year).

In truth, the sound quality of the original release was so mediocre that it was hard to tell exactly what the Fugs were ranting about. But when *The Fugs' First Album* was reissued in 1966, and climbed all the way to No. 142 on the US LP chart, the cuts were restored and the sonics improved. As a result, one could hear the unmistakeable sound of the line, 'Mmm, fug me like an angel' on the song 'Supergirl'; relish the throwaway remark, 'I'll give up heifer fucking' towards the end of 'My Baby Done Left Me'; and join in the chaotic singalong of 'Fucking nothing, sucking nothing' on the anthemic 'Nothing'. All this in the summer of 1966, when radio censors were only just waking up to the possibility that pop songs might be starting to include references to illegal drugs.

Within two or three years, the F-word would become an under-ground rock cliché, as common as the protestations of undying teenage love on the pop charts. And thanks to Norman Mailer's almost-but-not-quite rendering into print of the same forbidden letters, the path was cleared for 'fuck' to take its place at the heart of American literature.

Mailer's verbal invention prompted one of the most famous anecdotes in post-war American literature. A woman of great social stature – some sources say it was the actress Tallulah Bankhead, others the wit Dorothy Parker – is supposed to have sidled up to the author at a cocktail party, and accosted him like this: 'So – you're the young man who can't spell fuck?'

Messing with America's Mind

For more than fifty years, satirist and radical activist Paul Krassner has been pricking the sensitivities of every part of the American establishment. Like Jonathan Swift before him, Krassner specialises in extending an argument so far beyond the bounds of absurdity that even his most philosophically coherent opponents are forced to confront the full repercussions of their sacred cows and heart-felt beliefs.

His primary vehicle for this assault on pomposity, repression, and stupidity was, for many years, a magazine entitled *The Realist*. Its most notorious stunt involved the publication of what was presented as a deleted section from William Manchester's 'official' chronicle of the assassination of President John F. Kennedy. So accurate was Krassner's pastiche that thousands of readers came to believe *The Realist*'s account, which involved JFK's successor, Lyndon B. Johnson, taking sexual advantage of the late president's corpse.

An earlier escapade was simpler, arguably more tasteful, but every bit as effective. At a Fourth of July party in 1963, Krassner was offered a poster design for the magazine by a friend, featuring (as he recalled) 'the word FUCK in red-white-and-blue lettering emblazoned with stars and stripes. Now he needed a second word, a noun that would serve as an appropriate object for that verb.' The designer suggested AMERICA, which Krassner rejected as being both too obvious and also unfair: 'I was well aware that I probably couldn't publish *The Realist* in any other country.'

Yet this was a land which still, years after the madness of McCarthyism, lived in terror of any taint of Marxism. Krassner recalled reading the comments of pop singer Pat Boone at a recent anti-Communist rally in New York: 'I would rather see my four daughters shot before my eyes that have them grow up in a Communist United States. I would rather see those kids blown into heaven than taught into Hell by the Communists.' (For once, reality was more surreal than Krassner's imagination.)

What better, then, than for the poster to read FUCK COMMUNISM? The design was enacted in vivid red, with hammers and sickles adorning the lettering. Unable to find an engraver who would prepare a plate of the design for the pages of *The Realist*, Krassner decided to offer 'full-size color copies by mail. And if the post office interfered, I would have to accuse them of being soft on communism.'

It was a classic Krassner manoeuvre, pitting two American obsessions – anti-Communism and censorship of obscenity – at each other's throats. As he had hoped, the consequences were chaotic, as the same authorities who shared the poster's disdain for Communism were forced to censor it just the same. And, typically, Krassner decided to push the saga one step further, inventing the perfect anecdote to illustrate the stupidity of the moral outrage he had concocted:

Prohibitions

'At a Midwestern college, one graduating student held up a
FUCK COMMUNISM! poster as his class was posing for the
yearbook photograph. Campus officials found out and insisted
that the word FUCK be air-brushed out. But then the poster would
read: COMMUNISM! So that was air-brushed out too, and the
yearbook ended up publishing a class photo that showed this
particular student holding up a blank poster.'

You won't be surprised to learn that *The Realist* was also the
first 'underground' paper in America that dared to commit the
F-word to print. It emerged in a March 1960 interview with
psychologist Albert Ellis, who offered an insanely sensible suggestion about the usage of this forbidden word: 'My premise is that
sexual intercourse, copulation, fucking or whatever you wish to
call it, is normally, under almost all circumstances, a damned good
thing. Therefore, we should rarely use it in a negative, condemna-
tory manner.' Instead of saying 'fuck you', Ellis noted, we should
surely say 'unfuck you'. He concluded: 'Lots of times these words
are used correctly, as when you say, "I had a fucking good time."
That's quite accurate, since fucking, as I said before, is a good
thing; and a good thing leads to a good time. But by the same
token you should say "I had an *un*fucking *bad* time."' After which,
distinguished psychologist or not, a number of *Realist* readers
immediately cancelled their subscriptions, proving that not every
disgusted person lives in Tunbridge Wells.

There Are Four Letters in 'Howl'

More than 450 years after the four-letter word first appeared in
print, it still had the power to provoke police raids and obscenity
trials. In the case of Allen Ginsberg's epic poem 'Howl', there was
no shortage of provocative material from which to choose: 'cock',

'balls', and 'cunt' were among the words crammed into this lustrous assault on American conformism and bourgeois literary conventions. But there was no doubt which image prompted customs officials in New York to seize a consignment of Ginsberg's first publication, or persuaded an undercover cop in San Francisco to arrest the manager of a bookstore for selling him a copy.

Like his peers, poets or otherwise, Ginsberg casually bandied around all the variants of 'fuck' in his conversation and (as his collected correspondence proves) in letters to his friends. But he was more wary of echoing this freedom in print, as he weighed up the liberation on which he insisted as a writer, against the feverish conservatism of America in the early 1950s.

When he circulated copies of his 1952 poem 'A Crazy Spiritual', several key words – at least one of them doubtless beginning with the letter 'f' – were replaced by asterisks to avoid confronting the law. By the end of 1954, he was prepared to include the word 'fucking' in his poem 'Over Kansas', though it remained unpublished. So entwined was the desire for unfettered speech with the free-rolling rhythm of his versifying, however, that it was inevitable that his masterpiece, 'Howl', would push all limits of decency aside. Yet when Ginsberg was asked by fellow poet Lawrence Ferlinghetti to prepare a manuscript of 'Howl' and other works for publication by the City Lights Press in early 1956, Ginsberg kept one foot on each side of the fence.

The line that terrified the censors and guardians of the public morals was one that was guaranteed to raise a mixture of whoops and chuckles when Ginsberg read 'Howl' in public: 'who let themselves be fucked in the ass by saintly motorcyclists' – inspired, perhaps, by Ginsberg's infatuation with the image of Marlon Brando clad in biker leathers on the set of *The Wild One*. The line's combination of obscenity and homosexuality triggered every alarm bell the American establishment could erect to protect its culture.

Yet the man who could unashamedly deliver that line in front of college poetry groupies and Californian bohemians baulked at including a second profanity in the first edition of 'Howl': for decades thereafter, there was an enigmatic (but hardly unintelligible) reference in the poem to 'mother' being 'finally ******'. In readings, the omitted word began with an 'f', completing an image with Oedipal resonances. On the page, Ginsberg was clearly prepared to countenance men being ****** by motorcyclists; but not a mother, under any circumstances.

This did not prevent his book being the subject of a San Francisco obscenity trial in 1957, from which it emerged triumphant, with the F-word proclaimed legal as long as the work that contained it was of 'redeeming social importance'.

Once liberated from the shackles of national outrage, Ginsberg proceeded to demolish all remaining taboos in his work. In 1965, he became the first man to declaim the word 'fuck' on the stage of London's Royal Albert Hall, during a reading of 'The Change'. Within a decade of the 'Howl' trial, he was proudly reciting poems such as 'Please Master', in which he assumed the role of a subservient beneath the mighty rod of his lover. He described the encounter in such graphic detail that the piece could be used as an explanatory text for any visiting aliens anxious to grasp the mechanics of male homosexuality. But what would mother have thought?

Brooklyn Depths

Homosexual rape, extreme violence, male prostitution, vivid depiction of heroin addiction: just some of the passing attractions of Hubert Selby's remarkable story-sequence, *Last Exit to Brooklyn*: ruled legal after a 1964 trial in America, but banned in the altogether more prudish British climate in 1966, until the book was freed for publication on appeal two years later.

Amid the carefree splash of bodily fluids and the trampling of vital organs beneath muggers' boots, it was possible to overlook Selby's equally casual attitude towards the usage of the F-word. The first four pages of *Last Exit To Brooklyn* found Selby coining a succession of new variants on a common theme, with 'fuckin' (no apostrophe amid the carnage) followed by 'what-a-fuckin-load', 'whatthefuck', 'fuckaround' and 'fuckerself'. Having established that he could invent vernacular speech as easily as he could condemn his characters to lives of agonising torture, Selby resumed a more orthodox attitude towards his obscenities, letting Brooklyn's depravity speak for itself.

No 'F' in Peace

You can always rely upon a 'barefoot poet'. The Berkeley campus of the University of California was, in the early Sixties, the focus of the Free Speech Movement, which was a central stimulus in the formation of what became known as the 'counter-culture'. And it was in Berkeley, inevitably, that the poet John Thomson cast off his shoes on 2 March 1965, and sat on the steps of the student union building with a small white card pinned to his shirt. It carried a simple message, in his own handwriting: 'Fuck'. When Free Speech Movement leader Mario Savio playfully chided Thomson for being unclear, as 'fuck' could represent any of a range of parts of speech, Thomson adjusted his card accordingly. It now read: 'Fuck (verb)'.

This was, Thomson insisted, a protest against the war in Vietnam: mild-mannered, you might think, given the gamut of revolutionary behaviour exhibited by American outlaws during the halcyon years of the anti-war movement. Within an hour, however, Thomson had been arrested on a charge of breaching the peace, although he had not said a word, or attempted to organise a single soul to join his protest.

Thus began what one wit dubbed the 'Berkeley Filthy Speech Movement'. In the resulting furore, the president of the university was driven to resign after criticism of his heavy-handedness in allowing the arrest to take place; only to withdraw his resignation almost at once. Meanwhile, his board enforced the closure of an unofficial students' magazine, *Spider*, which had reported the incident under the rather clever headline: 'TO KILL A FUCKINGBIRD'.

Yet beyond Berkeley there was disappointment among national student leaders that the local radicals had failed to muster significant support for Thomson's subtle crusade; whereas some Free Speech Movement veterans felt that the 'fuck' controversy had distracted focus from their more far-reaching political manifesto. It was still possible in 1965 for young Americans to believe that the issue of Vietnam did not really concern them, a state of innocence that would soon be ended by President Johnson's intensification of American military involvement.

Such media coverage as there was of the affair tended to concentrate on the 'obscenity' of Thomson's card, rather than the motive for his protest. The specialist journal *Sexual Freedom* reported what had happened, which led the United States Postal Service to declare that this otherwise rather academic paper was 'an obscene publication'. Now, at last, Thomson's spark flared into something approaching a fire, as students and academics combined in San Francisco to form the League for Sexual Freedom around the offending journal. There was a mass meeting of support at San Francisco State University; then a naked swim-in against the war and in favour of unfettered use of four-letter words that described sexual intercourse. A Berkeley student was arrested for reading a pertinent extract from D.H. Lawrence's novel *Lady Chatterley's*

Lover in public, despite the fact that the book was now on sale legally in the United States.

Warned before a Berkeley reading that he would be arrested if he uttered any obscenities, beat poet Gary Snyder sent out a carefully worded statement to the local press. 'I have been hearing in the past two weeks that "fuck" in any usage is profane, dirty and obscene. Those who say this are the ones who make it so. Those who are genuinely disturbed by the word "fuck" – and its sister, "cunt" – the two most tabooed words in Standard English – I feel sorry for.'

This gentle crusade slowly spread across America – the first whisper, in fact, of the sexual revolution that would soon be howling around the Western world. By 1966, the League for Sexual Freedom was manufacturing its own memorabilia, to raise funds for the cause. Those who wanted to show solidarity within their homes or crash-pads could buy a poster that declared: 'Fuck for Peace'. And, as wearing a badge with that slogan would risk attracting the attention of the police, the League's members could exhibit their allegiance with a much more genteel message: 'Copulate for Coexistence'. Which somehow sounds much ruder than the alternative.

Fortunately for the concerned citizens of America, the police did not let these antics disturb their crusade to rid the nation of the four-letter word. In May 1967, cops in Ann Arbor, Michigan entered the offices of the underground newspaper *The Sun* (no relation), in the hope of discovering something illegal. While poking fun at the disgracefully long hair of the male staff, one policeman noticed, semi-concealed at the back of the room, a kite bearing the design of the Stars and Stripes – and, crucially, the slogan: 'Fuck America – go fly a kite'. He pulled it down, held it up to view it more closely, and declared that it could now be seen from the road, which broke a local ordinance prohibiting the display of obscene drawings within public view. The result: a court summons for editor and poster designer Gary Grimshaw, a fine of $150 and a sentence of fifteen days' imprisonment, with a year's probation to follow. *The Sun* duly reported the outcome under the restrained headline: 'Lady Justice Sodomized'.

It's Only Natural

From an article in the underground newspaper *Spokane Natural* in August 1967:

> CENSORSHIP
> We will try a test case.
> Fuckfuckfuckfuckfuckfuckfuckfuckfuckfuckfuckfuckfuck.
> This is to prove something. There is no redeeming social merit. Neither are your prurient interests to be aroused. In San Francisco once I saw a three minute movie with the word 'fuck' displayed every frame and nothing else, sixteen times a second, three minutes. In two minutes the audience was rocking with laughter. You can take fear of sex only so far.
> I don't expect anyone to say anything about these dirty words, thank you.

The response of the local community in Spokane was not verbal but physical: unidentified gunmen shattered the windows of the paper's offices.

A Vicar Speaks

'I think it's quite desirable to say "fuck". But not on the air, because there would be a number of complaints. I once got a letter from

a vicar who suggested that I should be castrated and deported for allowing a man to say "fuck" on the radio.'
(John Peel, 1971)

Mothers with Attitude

Parental Discretion Is Advised, declared one of the titles on NWA's debut album, *Straight Outta Compton*; and they weren't kidding. The California hip-hop quintet (whose initials disguised their true identity as Niggaz With Attitude) stoked governmental disquiet and rabid calls for censorship with the most memorable song on the album: rendered on the album sleeve as 'F--- Tha Police', but instantly recognisable via its rather more controversial chorus. It was hardly a subtle lyric; but then the scenario didn't call for subtlety, as the song documented police harassment of young black kids on the streets of Los Angeles. Rapper MC Ren boasted that he was 'a sniper with a hell of a scope/Takin' out a cop or two, they can't cope with me'; and he might as well have declared war on the USA, given the ferocity of the reaction from the authorities.

An assistant director of the FBI wrote to NWA's record label, deploring the popularity of the song, and warning them that 'advocating violence and assault is wrong'. Police officers refused to provide security for the crew's shows, some of which were cancelled. NWA were targeted for strip-searches in airports. Worse, there was even a backlash against the band within the black community, where they were excoriated for the misogyny of their lyrics and their promulgation of 'gangster' stereotypes. But their self-professed outlaw image proved to be more enduring, and NWA are widely credited as the forefathers of 'gangsta rap'.

Meanwhile, NWA proved to have too much attitude to contain

within one ensemble, and within a year of 'Fuck Tha Police' reaching the streets, one of their number, Oshea Jackson (better known as Ice Cube) was gone. While his ex-colleagues continued to chronicle the vicissitudes of urban life (sample titles included 'Findum, Fuckum & Flee', and 'I'd Rather Fuck You'), Ice Cube unleashed a scabrous assault on those he had left behind, 'No Vaseline', accusing them of hypocrisy and racial treachery, and their white manager of fraud. In retrospect, it is unfortunate that Cube chose to complain that NWA stalwart Eazy-E's 'dick is smelling like MC Ren's shit', given that E died of AIDS a few years later. But Cube was too angry to be profound, his rant's title explained by a key line: 'you're getting fucked out your green [cash] by a white boy, with no Vaseline'. Which is how 'fucked with no Vaseline' ended up in Jonathon Green's three-volume *Dictionary of Slang*, with Ice Cube credited as bringing the phrase into popular usage. In this instance, however, 'popular usage' seems to extend no further than the Vaseline reference turning up in another hip-hop piece, Boondox's 'Watch Your Step'.

What the Sister Saw

So Holden Caulfield is walking around his sister's school like an archetypal troubled teen – the kind of kid who, in the twenty-first century, would lay waste to everything around him with a rifle. But in *The Catcher in the Rye*, J.D. Salinger's 1951 novel, Holden merely finds 'something that drove me crazy . . . I thought how Phoebe and all the other little kids would see it, and how they'd wonder what the hell it meant, and then some dirty kid would tell them – all cockeyed naturally – what it meant, and how they'd all think about it and maybe even worry about it for a couple of days.' Caulfield even fantasises about catching up with the kid who was responsible for it, and smashing his head 'till he was good and goddam dead and bloody'.

So what is the outrageous object that makes Holden so crazy? Well, if you were reading this book in Britain at any time between its first publication in 1951, and the 1980s – a period in which it must have sold as many as a million copies – you'll know that what gets Holden's goat is some graffiti on the school wall that reads simply: '– you'. And that dash conceals an act of censorship that seemed to pass unnoticed, while the absence of that censorship aroused outrage even stronger than Holden's in Salinger's native land.

For the American edition of *The Catcher in the Rye*, just three years after Norman Mailer's 'fug' extravaganza in *The Naked and The Dead*, boldly quoted the school-wall inscription in full: 'fuck you'. It was hardly gratuitous obscenity: Caulfield is as upset as any censor, and when he finds the same phrase elsewhere in the school, he tries vainly to rub it out before any more kids can see it. For him, it's a symbol of the loss of innocence that awaits Phoebe – that awaits us all – when she is inexorably forced to take her place within the crushing corporatism of modern America.

The British publishers, Hamish Hamilton in hardback and Penguin for the paperback, didn't signpost their censorship: they evidently felt that the F-word could not be published in the UK, and reacted appropriately. The phrase was also snipped in many European translations, such as the Dutch, German, and Norwegian editions, while less abrasive language replaced the evil 'fuck' elsewhere. Little, Brown and Company in New York were altogether more courageous: in retrospect it's remarkable that the novel should not only have remained on the shelves during the height of the McCarthyism era, but also entered many school libraries and reading lists.

Throughout the Fifties, however, there were frequent efforts in the US to have *The Catcher in the Rye* banned, on both a local and national level. When the would-be censors were put on the spot, their general objections to the book's 'moral tone', 'juvenile delinquency' and 'Communist ethos' boiled down to one major problem: foul language. And as 'fuck you' was the only phrase that could possibly have triggered that reaction, it was clearly the presence of the F-word – even in reportage – that was the problem. As critic Jerome Beatty wrote in the *Saturday Review*, 'Banning [*Catcher*] from reading lists and then arguing over it has helped immeasurably to keep it going as one of the best-selling novels of the post-war years'. But several teachers and librarians apparently lost their jobs over their insistence on making Salinger's book available to its intended audience. Kids loved it; parental objections were summed up in one comment from a father: 'I don't want my girl studying this crap.'

Ronald Reagan for President

It was a small pamphlet, only a few pages long, its cover printed in a rather garish red, white, and blue. The centre of the design was a primitive rendering of the Stars and Stripes, with the logo 'Bean Spasms' circling it in cartoonish script. The remainder of the cover was filled with typescript, intended to resemble a Sixties computer print-out. It identified the author, J.G. Ballard; and the title: *Why I Want to Fuck Ronald Reagan*. In 1968, it featured in a court case that ruined a small publisher and bookshop owner; two years later, its inclusion in another book caused several thousand copies to be pulped.

For anyone remotely familiar with Ballard's trajectory through the Sixties, it was obvious that this short prose work was unlikely to be a pornographic tribute to the charms of the Governor of

California, who was preparing for his first presidential run. Ballard had surfaced in public awareness as a science fiction writer, but soon abandoned even the loose confines of SF for the border-free territory of speculative fiction. Its title aside, none of the pseudo-scientific language in *Fuck Ronald Reagan* could remotely be described as obscene. The 'story' masqueraded as a psychologist's report on the potency of Reagan's name and image, as measured by the response of an imaginary audience when confronted with the juxtaposition of the Governor and (to quote one example) the savage violence enacted by an automobile accident.

The only narrative in the tale was provided by two sentences, broken into section headings: 'During these assassination fantasies Tallis became increasingly obsessed with the pudenda of the Presidential contender mediated to him by a thousand television screens. The motion picture studies of Ronald Reagan created a scenario of the conceptual orgasm, a unique ontology of violence and disorder.' No fuel for masturbatory thrills there: merely food for thought about the ambiguous nature of the man who would assume the presidency in 1980.

Twelve years earlier, Ballard gave the piece to the owner of the Unicorn Bookshop in Brighton, Bill Butler, who operated a small press from the premises. The combination of a minor drugs bust and the Unicorn's reputation for stocking underground literature and magazines inspired the Sussex constabulary to mount a plain-clothes visit to the Unicorn in January 1968. A day later, they returned, and seized a vast quantity of books and journals that they felt were illegal under the Obscene Publications Act of 1959.

Among them were copies of the Ballard story, which attracted the particular outrage of the magistrates when the case came to trial that August. 'Is this not the meandering of a dirty and diseased mind?' one of them asked an expert witness who was testifying as to Ballard's literary stature. Ultimately, *Why I Want to Fuck*

Ronald Reagan had to be omitted from the list of 'obscene' publications found at the Unicorn, on a legal technicality. Nonetheless Bill Butler was convicted, fined £400, and ordered to pay all the legal costs – a burden that effectively capsized his business, and sent him to an early death.

Meanwhile, Ballard submitted the Reagan story to his book publishers in 1970, as part of a volume called (in Britain) *The Atrocity Exhibition* and (in America) *Love & Napalm, Export USA*. It took its place alongside other equally inventive uses of celebrity image, including several pieces hinged around the two Kennedy assassinations. The UK publication passed off without major incident, but in the USA, after copies had been printed, executives at Doubleday halted distribution and the entire first edition was pulped. Only two years later did the Grove Press, who had already defied the censors with editions of *Lady Chatterley's Lover* and *Naked Lunch*, enable the uncut text to reach the US market.

There was, according to Ballard, a strange postscript to the tale of *Why I Want to Fuck Ronald Reagan*. 'At the 1980 Republican Convention', he wrote, 'a copy of my Reagan text, minus its title and the running sideheads, and furnished with the seal of the Republican Party, was distributed to delegates. I'm told it was accepted for what it resembled, a psychological position paper on the candidate's subliminal appeal, commissioned from some maverick think-tank.' It's an enticing story; but also such a perfectly Ballardian incident, that one can't help wondering whether Ballard invented it, as part of an altogether larger psychological study of the gullibility of readers, critics, and academics – a way of ensuring an afterlife for the most controversial pages of his remarkable career.

Another prominent figure of 1968, Black Power activist Eldridge Cleaver, hit upon a much easier way to take Reagan's name in vain. Recently freed on bail after being charged with murdering a policeman, Cleaver was invited by the University of California to give a lecture about the Black Panther Party. When the Governor of California criticised this decision, Cleaver retaliated by asking five thousand students at a protest rally to chant: 'Fuck Ronald Reagan'. I wonder how many of them voted for Reagan when he was finally elected President in 1980 . . .

Imposters

Love in Middle Age

How did Ye Olde Timers – blokes like Shakespeare, Chaucer and Dr Johnson – talk about F-wording without using the F-word? Here are some of the terms that were at their disposal.

COVER: Used primarily of animals, presumably because the male 'covered' the female from view. Humans have the option of doing it the other way around.

FELTER: Alias 'to couple'. Doesn't imply that he 'felter' first, sadly for those wanting foreplay.

GOLEHEAD: A noun, as far as I can tell, with merry origins; might be usefully revived today to describe a man who insists on watching the football while he's at it.

GROPE UNDER GORE: This is not a summary of *Saw 2* or a follow-up to *Hostel*, but a way of suggesting that our distant ancestors liked to combine their resources without removing all their clothes, a 'gore' being a form of skirt and our ancestors not smelling too hot with their kit off.

HUMP: In the eighteenth century this term for fornication was regarded as virtually obsolete, but it made an unexpected recovery in the twentieth century, though its semi-humorous connotations have largely been superseded by the much more modern 'bonk'.

JAPE (or sometimes IAPE): Another verb meaning 'copulate', from Middle English, which survives in the language as a noun meaning a jolly adventure.

MEDDLE: It might suggest somebody fumbling about where he or she shouldn't be fumbling, but it actually refers to the full act of intercourse, from a Middle English word for coupling.

OCCUPY: This puts the global political movement of recent years into an entirely different perspective. Its origin seems obvious: one partner 'occupies' a place in the other. But the long-distant roots of the verb suggest a form of coupling rather than an invasion.

PILT: One of many Middle English verbs meaning thrust which were transferred to the sexual act in the age before foreplay.

PLAY UNDER CLOTH: There was no central heating in medieval times, so it was advisable to keep as many clothes on as possible.

PUTAGE: Sex as performed by a woman; note the link to the French 'putain', meaning whore, suggesting that a woman indulging in putage might be suspected of getting paid for it, or otherwise (worse still) actually enjoying it.

QUIFF: Can there possibly be a link between the seventeenth- and eighteenth-century use of this word to denote sexual intercourse, and its nineteenth-century emergence as a raised section of hair – one erection inspiring another, perhaps?

RAGE: With its associated noun, 'ragynge'; it doesn't mean that one or more partner is angry, merely that at least one of them is getting a bit carried away.

RIDE: Still used as a euphemism today, as in the Sixties R&B hit 'Ride Your Pony'.

ROGER: First Roger was a name; then 'roger' was the slang word for a penis; and then there was a verb to illustrate one of the things you can do with a penis.

SAM: Another Middle English verb meaning 'to couple'. 'Sam Roger' was probably the perfect porn star name for the sixteenth century.

SCREW: It implies a circular motion (see 'swive') and some use of force (see 'sting' and 'pilt'), which probably explains why this verb is still in use today.

SHAG: It's a bird, a dance, a repeated motif in the Austin Powers movies and – in Britain, of course – a just about socially acceptable word for a 'fuck'. American innocence about this term continues nonetheless, resulting in such marvellous CD titles as *Music to Shag By*.

STING: Which otherwise means 'to stab'. Women expecting an orgasm should maybe look elsewhere.

SWINK: In common use during the middle centuries of the last millennium. Its origin is the Old English verb 'swink', meaning toil or labour, which suggests that we have more fun in bed than they did 600 years ago. Chaucer uses this word in *The Reeve's Tale*.

SWIVE (or, often, SWYVE): Another mid-millennium favourite, which was perhaps as familiar to the world of 1500 and 1600 as 'fuck' is to us today. The origin is the Middle English verb 'swifan', which has also given us the modern word 'swivel', as it denotes movement in a circular fashion. Sex tips from the Middle Ages, boys and girls . . .

TREAD: Not as violent as it sounds, this referred only to coupling, not to trampling on one's partner afterwards.

TUP: Used primarily of animals. Not related to Tupperware parties, except in farming circles.

Poor Fanny Adams

When her grieving parents erected an ornate and majestic headstone over the grave of their eight-year-old daughter Fanny Adams in 1867, they can hardly have imagined that her name would become familiar to millions: first as a cruel euphemism, and then more enduringly as a substitute for one of the ruder phrases in the language. We can only be grateful that they did not live to see their girl forgotten, but her name taken in vain around the English-speaking world.

The circumstances of her death are too appalling to be described in detail. On a summer Saturday afternoon, Fanny was sent off to play in the meadows near her Hampshire home with two girls of a similar age. They were approached by a young clerk, who enticed the girls with halfpennies to accompany him – there being no concept of 'stranger danger' in the 1860s. He picked blueberries for them, all the while weighing up the choice that fate had presented to him. Two of the girls were sent safely away with the coins; Fanny happily accepted his invitation to stay. Then he carried her into a hop field, beat her to death with a stone, and proceeded to dismantle her body, spreading her vital organs over a wide area; some parts of the corpse were never located. In his diary, he wrote simply: 'Killed a young girl. It was fine and hot.' (He claimed he had been acting as a reporter, and meant to write: 'Killed: a little girl.' But nobody believed him.) As he had made little effort to conceal his guilt, he was quickly caught, and hanged for murder on Christmas Eve.

So notorious was the crime that Fanny's name remained in the public memory; and quickly entered into the realms of black humour. Any particularly ghastly meat dish was soon likely to be described (in coarse company) as looking like Fanny Adams, and her name became attached to the undesirable meat rations offered to lower ranks in the Royal Navy. Time changes words and their meaning, and by the end of the century Sweet Fanny Adams was no longer an unappetising meat dish, but an all-purpose nickname for anything of no great value – at which point Fanny Adams and the phrase 'fuck all' became entangled, by virtue of their shared initials, and 'sweet FA' became a polite abbreviation for them both. But Fanny's gravestone is still visible at the cemetery in Alton, in memory of what must be the cruellest innovation in the history of the English language.

*Saying F**k Without Saying F**k*

BLANK: Quite common in nineteenth-century writing, though not in refined conversation, the word 'blank' was employed as an all-purpose tool of invective and obscenity, leaving the identity of the omitted (or blank) word to the imagination of the audience. So, in theory, a nineteenth-century novelist of the 1800s could have allowed one of his characters to say 'I blanking well hope that he gives more of a blank than he blanking well did last time' – though he probably wouldn't have attracted any readers. Given that 'blank' was most commonly employed as a substitute for 'fuck', it is mildly amusing that one of the most popular British television game shows of the Eighties was titled *Blankety-Blank*; and more amusing that most of its viewers didn't realise that the BBC programme they were watching was named after a string of expletives.

BLEEP: The twentieth-century equivalent of 'blank', named after the tendency for broadcasters to hide unwanted language on radio and television behind an electronic noise. Coming soon to BBC1: a game show entitled *Bleepity-Bleep*.

CHUCK: Though it rhymes with the F-word, and might therefore lend itself to easy exclamations of 'chuck off', this particular C-word only seems to have entered the dictionary of dirty talk in one phrase: 'Chuck you, Farly'. Which, as any relatives of the late Reverend Dr Spooner will instantly realise, is a playful inversion of a wartime expression (First World War, in fact), 'Fuck you, Charlie'. The latter phrase is often aimed at 'Jack' instead of 'Charlie', but somehow 'Juck you, Fack' doesn't roll off the tongue in the same way.

EFF: This is almost as varied as the F-word itself, extending easily into exclamations ('eff off!'), participles ('effing'), tenses ('effed'), adjectives (yep, we're 'effing' again) and extensions ('em-eff'). Delivered with sufficient venom, it can carry nearly as much force as the full effing expletive.

FLIP: Or rather 'flipping', as a way of intensifying a statement – in Britain, more often than not, applied to the state of the weather, and as mild an outburst as you can imagine. It was first applied as a substitute for 'fucking' in the nineteenth century, which was when use of the F-word and its derivatives among the English-speaking population appears to have boomed, and genteel disguises were therefore much in demand.

FRIG: Two sexual activities are captured in one word here, as 'frig' entered our language as a quick way of saying 'masturbation', and then within the last two hundred years invited others to join in by becoming an alternative for 'fuck' in the strictly sexual sense. 'Frigging' is sometimes heard as a description of intercourse, or as an intensifier ('frigging typical'). But 'frig off' merely sounds clumsy. It's safe to say that 'frig' was less safe to use in polite company in 1800 than it is today, when a large proportion of your audience won't know what you're talking about.

FUDGE: Fudge is to 'fuck' as sugar is to 'shit': polite, inoffensive, safe for work. Any number of words beginning with the crucial F will serve just as well – fiddlesticks, for example, though not forks.

NAFF: As expressed most vocally by Princess Anne in 1982, who surprised a group of royal photographers by asking: 'Why don't you just naff off?' The key elements of that phrase had entered mainstream British culture thanks to the TV sitcom *Porridge*. It was set in prison, where the language is not always as restrained as one might like, so to give the setting some sense of authenticity, there had to be some bad language in the air. Characters' repeated invitations to each other to 'naff off' satisfied that desire, without disturbing the horses or other members of the royal household. But like so many examples of vulgarity in the English language, 'naff' owes its origins to the services, specifically the Royal Air Force in the Second World War. It was revived briefly by novelist Keith Waterhouse in *Billy Liar*, and then lay dormant for more than a decade until it reappeared in the mouth of *Porridge* star Ronnie Barker in 1974.

SCREW: It works in some circumstances, but not others. 'Screw you!' is a genuinely cathartic release of anger and contempt, while 'screw' has long been an alternative way of describing sexual intercourse. In the latter sense, the word can be traced back to the Latin word for a sow, '*scrofa*', and thence to the fifteenth-century French word, '*escroue*'. Why a sow? Well, as we have had cause to mention elsewhere in this book, pigs have curly tails, and so the suggestion of any (how can I put this delicately?) circularity in the motion of two lovers brought to mind the action of, er, screwing a screw. Talking of which: a 'screw' in the seventeenth and eighteenth centuries was less likely to be the act of copulation, but someone for a man to copulate with – in other words, it was one of the many words available to describe a common strumpet or whore. Finally, returning to the use of 'screw' as a euphemism for the F-word, we find that it is distressingly limited: you could claim to be 'screwing annoyed', or call someone a 'screwer' in a moment of exasperation, but neither usage is likely to win you an argument.

WHO/WHAT THE . . . : Which leaves the unspeakable word
unspoken, and allows generous-minded people to think that
you were about to say 'who the hell?' or 'what the blazes?'. In
twenty-first-century social intercourse, 'WTF?' serves much the
same purpose.

Father Feck

So exactly how rude is the Irish word 'feck'? Brought to popular
acceptance in Great Britain via the TV sitcom *Father Ted*, 'feck' is
widely assumed (by the English, Scottish, and Welsh) to be an
invented substitute for the other F-word – presumably to enable
Channel 4 to avoid criticism from easily outraged viewers.

But 'feck' existed centuries before Father Jack and his litany of
'Feck! Arse! Drink!' Like 'fuck', it can be extended into a personal
noun ('fecker') and an adjective ('fecking', often with the 'g'
dropped). There is one major difference between the two words,
however. 'Fuck' suggests sexual intercourse; 'feck', at least in its
pre-Jack form, doesn't.

It exists, instead, as a word with three dominant meanings: to
throw something; to steal something; or as a term of exasperation
or abuse. The first two senses can trace their derivations back to
the Middle Ages; the last was surely inspired by the term's similarity
to the English subject of this book. In Ireland, at least, it is less
confrontational to tell someone to 'feck off' than it would be to
exchange that vital 'e' for a 'u'. It's more humorous, less pointed,
and more acceptable in polite society. But elsewhere, the Channel
4 effect is dominant: 'feck' might raise a smile among fellow aficio-
nados of *Father Ted*, but it is still a four-letter word, best left to
those who – like Father Jack – have profound intoxication as an
excuse.

F**k

FCUK

Bus drivers in Vancouver must have been very sensitive. In March 2000, they successfully lobbied to have advertisements for the French Connection brand removed from their vehicles. The problem? The ads featured the company's internationally notorious abbreviation, 'FCUK'. Its presence, even in small print, so the drivers alleged, amounted to sexual harassment in the workplace. Rather than fight an embarrassing court case, their management agreed to impose a ban on the 'FCUK' campaign.

The story seems to beg the hashtag 'political correctness gone mad'. But beyond the gentle souls who courageously operate public transport in Canada, the 'FCUK' logo (an abbreviation of French Connection UK) raised much larger issues about censorship around the world. The company had been flourishing for twenty-five years when, in 1997, advertising guru Trevor Beattie was invited to maximise its awareness among the public. And so was born an eight-year campaign that pushed the boundaries of public decency to the limit, and divided its viewers between those who were outraged and those who were simply amused.

The original slogan was itself double-edged: 'fcuk fashion'. The clever – or annoying, depending on your point of view – allusion to the four-letter word was launched on posters and billboards, and was soon transplanted into press ads and onto T-shirts. Within a year – a timeframe in which FCUK's profits in Britain increased by 88 per cent – almost every aspect of the French Connection brand had been refashioned to include the contro-versial logo. Customers could choose from shirts proclaiming 'too busy to fcuk', 'hot as fcuk', and (in Australia, naturally) 'no fcuking worries'.

In retrospect, what's remarkable is how quickly the 'fcuk' gimmick was accepted. There was harrumphing from expected quarters, and a general feeling among people over a certain age that, really, while we are very broad-minded, this is taking things too far, and in any case, what about the influence this will have on our children? But the campaign and the posters continued without interference from the authorities, even when French Connection marked December 1998 with a 'FCUK Christmas' slogan. If pushed for an explanation of their cheeky behaviour, the company merely boasted that they had 'created attention and provoked discussion'.

The new year began with British boxing champion Lennox Lewis sporting the 'FCUK' logo on his shorts in a world heavyweight title fight against Evander Holyfield. When trouble came, it was from an unexpected quarter: another business claiming the right to the website address fcuk.com. There was a court case, inevitably, at which French Connection's lawyers asked for a sign of 'goodwill' from their opponents. This riled the judge, Mr Justice Rattee, who matched up to his name: 'How can you talk about goodwill in connection with such a tasteless and obnoxious campaign? Fcuk is just a euphemism for the obscene expletive fuck. It may be you have been hoist by your own petard in using such an extraordinary advertising slogan.' To which FC's lawyer, Mary Vitoria, replied: 'Your lordship might find it offensive. I might find it offensive. But young people who buy clothes do not find it offensive, they find it amusing.'

French Connection's profits seemed to suggest that she was right. But around the world, opposition to the campaign was slowly emerging. Products bearing the 'FCUK' logo were barred from many American stores. There was outrage in Singapore when the logo appeared on the side of buses. A British judge ordered a juror to go home when he wore a 'FCUK' T-shirt in court. Posters for French Connection's radio station, FCUK FM, were removed for making the link between 'fcuk' and 'fuck' too blatant, with their strapline: 'FCUK FM FROM PNUK TO RCOK AND BACK. NON-STOP FNUK. FCUK FM'.

By now, the Advertising Standards Authority were demanding that French Connection submit each new poster to them for approval, before it appeared on the streets – rather than waiting, as they usually did, for complaints from the public to arrive. Trevor Beattie mounted a stiff defence of the campaign: 'FCUK is an advertising idea which became a brand. The T-shirts have got us into more trouble than the advertising in terms of press coverage. Yet I never saw the advertising as offensive. When you think of what else is happening in the world it puts it all into perspective – it really isn't that important. But the facts speak for themselves: we used it in advertising; the ASA put us in the sin bin; we came out; we sinned again; we went back in . . . The thinking behind everything we have done for FCUK is about bending the rules, entertaining, subverting, doing something no clothes store should do. It's all been about building a tone of voice for the brand. It's about attitude – if you're a bit alternative or anti-establishment, FCUK is the brand for you.' But within a year, 'fcuk' had disappeared from French Connection's advertising campaigns, though it survives in the names of the company's range of perfumery, which includes both 'FCUK Him' and 'FCUK Her'. Now *that's* what I call fragrant.

The Final Word

Terry-Thomas – the name alone will bring a smile to the face of any filmgoer of a certain age. He may not have been the most versatile actor in cinema history – every role turned out pretty much the same – but his appearance on screen was a guarantee of humour. His archetypal portrayal was that of the English cad:

the bounder who isn't as posh as he thinks he is, and who isn't going to let any man, woman, or foreigner (especially the latter two categories) get one over on him.

In his twilight years, he struggled with Parkinson's disease, but clearly retained the Terry-Thomas style. His last recorded words were addressed to a waiter, who had fallen foul of the strict Terry-Thomas code of etiquette; and they are also a perfect way to sign off this F-word cavalcade: 'Fucking cheek'.

Appendix

FYFI

A 21st-Century Dictionary of Abbreviations

4Q – Fuck You
ACGAF – Absolutely couldn't give a fuck
AFDN – Any fucking day now
AFGO – Another fucking growth opportunity
AFT – About fucking time
AFU – All fucked up
AMF – Adios, motherfucker
AMIIGAF – Ask me if I give a fuck
ASAFP – As soon as fucking possible
ATFP – Answer the fucking phone
AUFM? – Are you fucking mental?
AYFKM? – Are you fucking kidding me?
AYFS? – Are you fucking serious?
BAMF – Badass motherfucker
BBAMFIC – Big badass motherfucker in charge
BBMFIC – Big bad motherfucker in charge
BFD – Big fucking deal

BFE – Bum fuck Egypt
BFR – Big fucking rock
BITFOB – Bring it the fuck on, bitch
BMF – Bad motherfucker (or, be my friend)
BTFO – Back the fuck off
BTFW – By the fucking way
BUFF – Big ugly fat fuck
CBF – Can't be fucked
CBFA – Can't be fucking arsed
CGAF – Couldn't give a fuck
CRAFT – Can't remember a fucking thing
CTFD – Calm the fuck down
CTFO – Come the fuck on; or, chill the fuck out
CTFU – Cracking the fuck up
DAFS – Do a fucking search
DF – Dumb fuck
DFC – Don't fucking care
DFL – Dead fucking last
DFU – Don't fuck up
DFWM – Don't fuck with me
DFWMT – Don't fucking waste my time
DGAF – Don't give a fuck
DILF – Dad I'd like to fuck
DILLIGAF? – Do I look like I give a fuck?
DYOFDW – Do your own fucking dirty work
EAPFS – Everything about Pittsburgh fucking sucks
ESADYFA – Eat shit and die, you fucking asshole
ESMF – Eat shit, motherfucker
ESYF – Eat shit, you fuck
FAH – Fucking-A hot
FAP – Fucking-A pissed
FA-Q – Fuck you

FAY – Fuck all, y'all

FB – Fuck-buddy

FBI – Fucking brilliant idea

FEITCTAJ – Fuck 'em if they can't take a joke

FFS – For fuck's sake

FI – Fuck it

FIF – Fuck, I'm funny

FIIK – Fucked if I know

FILF – Father I'd like to fuck

FINE – Fucked-up, insecure, neurotic, emotional

FKM – Fuck 'em

FLUID – Fucking look it up, I did

FMBB – Fuck me, baby

FMBO - Fuck my brains out

FMFLTH – Fuck my fucking life to hell

FML – Fuck my life

FMLTWIA – Fuck me like the whore I am

FMN – Fuck me now

FMUTA – Fuck me up the ass

FNG – Fucking new guy

FO – Fuck off

FOA – Fuck off, asshole

FOAD – Fuck off and die

FOAG – Fuck off and Google

FOMOFO – Fuck off, motherfucker

FRED – Fucking ridiculous electronic device

FSOB – Fucking son of a bitch

FSU – Fuck shit up

FTF – Fuck, that's funny

FTN – Fuck that noise

FTRF – Fuck, that's really funny

FTS – Fuck that shit

FTW – Fuck the world
FU – Fuck you
FU2 – Fuck you too
FUBAH – Fucked up beyond all hope
FUBAR – Fucked up beyond all recognition
FUBB – Fucked up beyond belief
FUBOHIC – Fuck you, bend over, here it comes
FUJIMO – Fuck you, Jack, I'm moving on
FUM – Fucked up mess
FWLF – Fuck work, let's fuck
FWOT – Fucking waste of time
FYFI – For your fucking information
FYIFV – Fuck you, I'm fully vested
FYRB – Fuck you right back
GAFC – Get a fucking clue
GAFL – Get a fucking life
GAGF – Go and get fucked
GFAD – Go fuck a duck
GFF – Go fucking figure
GFI – Good fucking idea
GFY – Go fuck yourself
GFYMF – Go fuck yourself motherfucker
GILF – Grandmother I'd like to fuck
GMAFB – Give me a fucking break
GTFA – Go the fuck away
GTFBTW – Get the fuck back to work
GTFO – Get the fuck out
GTFOOH – Get the fuck out of here
GTFU – Grow the fuck up
HFS – Holy fucking shit!
HTFU – Hurry the fuck up
IDFC – I don't fucking care

IDGAF – I don't give a fuck
IDGAFF – I don't give a flying fuck
IFU – I fucked up
IHNFC – I have no fucking clue
IHTFP – I hate this fucking place
IMFO – In my fucking opinion
IRDGAF – I really don't give a fuck
IWFU – I wanna fuck you
IYFD – In your fucking dreams
IWTFU – I want to fuck you
JAFO – Just another fucking onlooker
JAFS – Just another fucking salesman
JFDI – Just fucking do it
JFGI – Just fucking Google it
JFH – Just fuck him/her
KDFU – Kracking da fuck up
KMFA – Kiss my fucking ass
LAGNAF – Let's all get naked and fuck
LDIMEDILLIGAF – Look deeply into my eyes, does it look like I give a fuck?
LF – Let's fuck
LMFAO – Laughing my fucking ass off
LMMFAO – Laughing my motherfucking ass off
LOLWTF – Laughing out loud, 'What the fuck?'
MBRFN – Must be real fucking nice
MF – Motherfucker
MFIC – Motherfucker in charge
MILF – Mother I'd like to fuck
MOFO – Motherfucker
MPFB – My personal fuck buddy
MTFFBWU – May the fucking force be with you
NFC – No fucking chance

NFE – No fucking excuse
NFF – Not fucking fair
NFG – No fucking good
NFI – No fucking idea
NFW – No fucking way
NIYWFD – Not in your wildest fucking dreams
NNCIITFZ – Not now, chief, I'm in the fucking zone
OMFG – Oh my fucking God
PFC – Pretty fucking cold
PMFF – Pardon my fucking French
PFH – Pretty fucking hot
PFT – Pretty fucking tight
PTFO – Pass the fuck out
QFT – Quit fucking talking
RFN – Right fucking now
RFR – Really fucking rich
RFS – Really fucking soon
ROTFLMFAO – Rolling on the floor, laughing my fucking ass off
RTFM – Read the fucking manual
RTFQ – Read the fucking question
RTWFQ – Read the whole fucking question
RUFKM? – Are you fucking kidding me?
SAPFU – Surpassing all previous fuck-ups
SFTM – Stop fucking texting me
SFTTM – Stop fucking talking to me
SNAFU – Situation normal, all fucked up
STFU – Shut the fuck up
STFW – Search the fucking web
SUUFI – Shut up, you fucking imbecile
TARFU – Things are really fucked up
TFF – Too fucking funny
TFIF – Thank fuck it's Friday

Appendix

TFMIU – The fucking manual is unreadable
TFYS – The fuck you say
TIGAF? – Think I give a fuck?
TILF – Teacher I'd like to fuck
TTMF – Ta-ta, motherfucker
TYAFY – Thank you and fuck you
UFB – Un-fucking-believable
VFF – Very fucking funny
WAFB – What a fucking bitch
WAFM – What a fucking mess
WAFU – What a fuck up
WGAFF? – Who gives a flying fuck?
WITFITS? – What in the fuck is this shit?
WTF? – What (or Who) the fuck?
WTFDYJS? – What the fuck did you just say?
WTFGDA – Way to fucking go, dumbass
WTFH? – What the fucking hell?
WTFDYCM? – Why the fuck did you call me?
WTFWYCM? – Why the fuck would you call me?
WYFM? – Would you fuck me?
YAFA – Yet another fucking acronym
YATFM – You are too fucking much
YBF – You've been fucked

Discography

Don't Do That!

Songs with precise fucking instructions

'Don't Fuck My Sister' (7000 Dying Rats)
'Don't Fuck My Friends' (Raxx)
'Don't Fuck With My Kinfolk' (Pimpsta)
'Don't Fuck With the Babysitter' (Owleater)
'Don't Fuck With My Pooch' (No Redeeming Social Value)
'Don't Fuck With Greatniss' (N-PO$E)
'Don't Fuck With a Lyricist' (Let Go & Control!)
'Don't Fuck With Robert Smith' (Planetakis)
'Don't Fuck With the FBI' (Metaverse)
'Don't Fuck Giraffes!' (David Hahn)

Internet Dating Can Be a Tricky Business

Songs that suggest your blind date is fucked

'Let's Fuck Differently' (Elastic No-No Band)

'I Feel Like a Fat Frustrated Fuck' (The Evaporators)
'Fuck 'Em All, That's My Slogan' (Philthy Fingers)
'Fuck the Bastards of the Human Race' (Amy Honey & Nuclear Weasel)
'Any Cunt You Can Fuck I Can Fuck Better' (Shat)
'Big Massive Fuck-Off Attitude' (The Lollies)
'Fuck You Softly With a Chainsaw' (Levan & Rei Taak)
'Gut the Slut Before I Fuck' (Lividity)
'I Kill Everything I Fuck' (GG Allin)
'I'll Dig You Up and Fuck You' (CodeCracker)

The Doctor Will See You Now, Sir

Songs about fucked-up bodily functions

'Oh Fuck, I Feel So Down' (Dano TheCube)
'Ringworm Fuck' (Voetsek)
'Fuck My Eardrums' (TomWax & Franksen)
'Fuck My Liver' (Gut-shot)
'Fuck the Hiccups' (Beercan!)
'Blood Sucking Fuck' (Deathwitch)
'Cunt Pussy Fuck Shit' (Tourette's Funk Syndrome)
'Fuck My Shit Stinks' (Boxcar Cadavers)
'Prolapsed Trachea Fuck Toy' (Saprogenic)
'Fecal Stuffed Fuck Stumps' (Guttural Secrete)
'Severed Foot Fuck Fetish' (Eviscerated)
'Head Fuck Is Dead' (Randy)
'I'm Dying Danny, I Don't Give a Fuck About the Rules' (Chainsaw Murphy)
'The Doctor Called, Turns Out I'm Sick as Fuck' (Decade)

Appendix

And They Said Chivalry Was Dead

Songs that simply say 'Fuck you'

'Fuck You, Get a Job and Have a Nice Day' (Peter Wilde)
'For Your Information, Go Fuck Yourself' (Big Deformed Head)
'Fuck Is the Only Word For You' (Larry Pierce)
'Fuck You! Fuck You! Fuck You!' (The Jonny 3)
'You're Old, Fuck You' (Anal Cunt)
'I Reckon You Should Shut the Fuck Up' (Consolidated)
'I'm Pro-You-Shutting-the-Fuck-Up' (Another Breath)
'You Fuck Off First, Then I'll Fuck Off' (The Roman Line)
'Fuck Your Fuckin Fuck' (Pin-Up Godiva)
'I Can't Finger Fuck You If Your Pussy Stank' (Wolf Pack Click)
'Fuck You & The Cum-Soaked Bitch You Rode In On' (Iowa Beef
   Experience)

Would You Like Fries With That?

Songs that fuck with your appetite

'All You Can Fuck and Eat' (Prophecy)
'Fuck Your Pretzel' (Puffy Areolas)
'How to Fuck a Donut' (.tape.)
'Fuck the Bread, Eat Rice' (Byousatsu Endorphin)
'Fuck Rap, Eat Icecream' (Lautschrift)
'Ice Cream Apple Fuck' (Fight like Apes)
'Fuck Those Fries, I'm from Idaho' (9-Volt Tongue)
'Fuck Meat' (Noah Swords, King of the Deathmatch)
'Fuck the Rotted Meat' (Reprobation)
'Gentlemen Fuck Your Eggs' (JJ Star Duran)

F**k

'I Eat Fuck' (Daniel Jordan)
'Eat My Fuck' (Filthy Maggoty Cunt)
'Eat a Bowl of Fuck' (The Ugly Fat Kids)
'Eat Shit and Fuck a Moose' (Flesh Parade)

Drink Up, It's Time to . . .

Songs that tell you it's last fucking orders

'Drink, Fuck, Drive Truck' (The Tower of Dudes)
'Fuck You, Where's My Brew' (Dehumanized)
'Fuck Vodka, Drink Juice' (MrShada)
'Fuck Juice No. 9' (Reverse Dotty)
'Fuck Your Lemonade' (Ryan Arklin)
'Fuck You, I'm Drunk' (Bondo)
'Fuck! I'm Drunk!' (Poison Apples)
'Too Drunk to Fuck' (Dead Kennedys)
'There Are Cigarette Ashes in My Coffee and I Don't Give a Fuck'
    (Pat Kinsella)
'How to Fuck Up a Cup of Coffee' (Accidents Never Happen)

What Exactly Is It That You Don't Like About Me?

Songs that make it perfectly fucking clear

'Fuck Your Jacket' (All Teeth And Knuckles)
'Fuck Your Lifestyle' (Shotgun Shell)
'Fuck Your Cigarette' (UFO)
'Fuck Yr Obvious Words' (Racebannon)
'Fuck Your Mum' (Blank 183)

Appendix

'Fuck You, You're Irish' (Hub City Stompers)
'Fuck Your Nationality' (Disorder)
'Fuck Your Lyrics, Fuck Your Music' (Plastic Riot)
'Fuck Your Scene, Fuck Your Crew, Fuck You' (Slam Coke)
'Stop Sayin' Fuck All the Time!' (Lord Funk)

Basic Music-Biz P.R.

Songs designed to advance your fucking career

'Fuck Commercial Music' (Olive Oil)
'Fuck This Track' (Mark Frostbite)
'Fuck the Fans' (Bomb The Music Industry)
'Fuck Blvd Records' (Young Trigger)
'Fuck a Major Label' (Pistol)
'Fuck You Time Warner' (The Gozinyahs)
'Fuck Corporate Death' (Marta G. Wiley)
'Fuck the Rap Game' (M.O.B.)
'Fuck You and Your Record Contract' (The Punk Group)
'Fuck the Music Industry' (Death Before Disco)

Don't Sit on the Fence

Songs that mark your fucking ballot paper

'America, Fuck Your Freedom' (United Satanic Apache Front)
'Fuck Bush' (Entropia)
'Fuck Fascism' (The Oppressed)
'Fuck L'Oppression' (Baba)
'Fuck Peace' (K-Deejays)

'Fuck Racists' (Mac-Nut)
'Fuck the Bloody Euro' (Kick'M Ass)
'Fuck the British' (New DQT & The Dirty Shirtlifters)
'Fuck the Countryside Alliance' (Future Of The Left)
'Fuck the KKK' (The Pricks)
'Fuck the Nazis' (Zion Train & Neville Staples)
'Fuck the Tories' (Riot Squad)

Call Me Enigmatic

Songs that make you say 'WTF?'

'What the Fuck Is a Chinese Downhill?' (Racebannon)
'Fuck the Phenomena' (Chew Lay)
'Eloquent Carrot House Fuck Up' (Dejan Milicevic)
'Fear Is Our Crowd, Fuck Sauerkraut' (Disaster KFW)
'Fuck Gravity's Rainbow' (Drvgdealer)
'Fuck Dancing, Let's Economy' (Mut!ny)
'Fuck Lacan and Also Freud' (Svenson)
'Fuck Freud, Let's Smoke Cigars' (All Florida)
'Fuck Zhe Postmoderne' (Laufmasche)
'Fuck Pasteur, This Is Rage!' (Crossing the Rubicon)
'Thank You Cloud, Fuck You Deerfly' (Warmth)
'If You're Claudius, Who The Fuck Is Fortinbras?' (Jason Pickett)

Appendix

At the Zoo

Songs that say 'Never fuck with an animal'

'Animal (Fuck Like a Beast)' (W.A.S.P.)
'I Wanna Fuck a Bull' (Abimonistas)
'Fuck Bunny' (The Society Islands)
'Fuck Pitbull' (Nate The Great)
'The Shark's Own Private Fuck' (Sunny Day Real Estate)
'Fuck the Whales' (Infernal Torment)
'Fuck You and Your Cat' (Goldfinger)
'We Will Fuck Horses' (Gerard Baste)
'I'm Gonna Fuck Me a Moose' (Preschool Tea Party Massacre)
'Go Fuck Yourself with Your Cat on the Roof' (The Narcotic Daffodils)
'Die, You Big Fuck-Off Spider, Die' (The Ansion)

Sexual Healing

Songs about a fuck to remember

'Amazing Fuck' (Renee Golemba)
'The Perfect Ass Fuck' (Master/Slave Relationship)
'Four-Way-Fuck and Suck' (Meat Shits)
'Fuck U to Death' (Endgestalt)
'Another Poor Fuck' (GAS)
'Another Worthless Fuck' (Furnace)
'Fuck Me, Suck Me, Steal My Bike' (The Kings of Industry)
'Fuck, I Hope You're Not Pregnant' (Hostage Life)
'I Have No Idea How to Fuck' (Princess Party Mountain)
'Forced to Fuck Myself' (Witch Hat)

F**k

R.E.S.P.E.C.T.

Songs that ask: 'Who are you calling a fucking feminist?'

'Easy Going Girls Are Always One Fuck Away' (Secondsmile)
'I Wanna Fuck Me Some Hoes' (Mr Knightowl)
'Immoral Fucking Bitch' (Spam)
'Fuck This Biatch' (EmOne)
'Should I Fuck This Big Fat Ho?' (Blowfly)
'We Fuck Titties Everyday' (Brett Mounce)
'Fuck Her Up the Ass' (Mikey Galactic)
'Mike Fucks 300lb Fat Chicks Sober' (Fuck Face)
'I Never Fuck With Ugly Girl From Togo' (Chris Hope & Andre
    Walter)
'Beat the Fuck out of That Worthless Bitch' (Artery Eruption)
'Rape, Torture, Terminate & Fuck' (GG Allin)

Who Exactly Did You Have in Mind?

Songs that don't beat around the fucking bush

'I Wanna Fuck My Chick in The Skate Ditch' (Smogtown)
'I Wanna Fuck Britney Spears' (The Springfields)
'I Want to Fuck Lily Cole' (Zippy Kid)
'I Wanna Fuck Ted Nugent' (Fruit Pie)
'I Wanna Fuck Your Mom' (The Sleazies)
'I Wanna Fuck Your Dad' (Blowfly)
'I Want to Fuck Your Girlfriend' (Cancerslug)
'I Want to Fuck My Ex-Girlfriend's Friends' (Jeff Capo)
'I Wanna Fuck All the Girls in My School' (Bazooka)
'Granny I'd Like to Fuck' (Tatono)